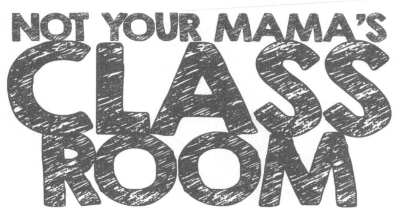

What You Need to Know as a Parent About Your Child's Digital Education

DR. WENDY L. OLIVER

LIFEWISE BOOKS

NOT YOUR MAMA'S CLASSROOM
WHAT YOU NEED TO KNOW AS A PARENT ABOUT YOUR CHILD'S DIGITAL EDUCATION
BY DR. WENDY L. OLIVER

Published by:

 LIFEWISE BOOKS

PO BOX 1072
Pinehurst, TX 77362
LifeWiseBooks.com

To contact the author | DrWendyOliver.com

ISBN (Print): 978-1-947279-93-3
ISBN (Ebook): 978-1-947279-94-0

DEDICATION

For Dan Long, who knows when to drive left, that the best offense is a good defense, when to set a screen, and when to draw a charge—because winning for him is about serving kids, not his personal ambition.

Thank you, Dan, for believing in me early in my career and allowing me to learn from you. Thank you for also managing the politics, so we could make a difference in so many students' lives.

CONTENTS

CHAPTER 1
YOUR LIFE AND HOMEWORK: THE REALITY SHOW

A DAY IN THE LIFE OF EVERY PARENT

So, it is now 8:30 pm, and dinner is cleaned up. When you ask if your child has finished his homework he says, "I don't know how to do it." Does this sound familiar? After you mumble comments under your breath about the "new way to do math" you decide to try and tackle the homework with your child.

When you ask to see the assignment, you get a blank stare and a story that goes something like...

Well, we did some sample problems in class, and she showed us some websites. I understood it then, but I don't really remember what we did.

Of course, you say something like, "Okay, get your book and bring me the worksheet she gave you, so we can look at it."

But…there aren't worksheets, and there isn't a textbook. Your child's teacher uses not just "new math," but also a new approach to teaching called a blended approach. Most everything is paperless, so how do you get information to help him?

I have found that most parents want to help their children succeed, but they need a common vocabulary with educators and tools to do so. This book will help guide you through the process of transition into a digital education. I will help you navigate from ways you may have learned in school (textbooks and desks in rows), to how your child is learning (digital classroom). If they aren't already, they will be using digital devices in the classroom and embracing technology to learn and collaborate on assignments and on projects.

Since I'm a parent and former educator, I will make a bold statement. Often, educators are very good at asking parents for support and complaining when they don't get it. However, educators don't always provide parents with the tools they need to help their children be successful with their own expectations, myself included. We assume that if kids know how to use a device, their parents must too. We all make the mistake and assume that if kids know how to use their smartphones, then they are fluent in digital literacy and will immediately know how to use devices for academic purposes with no additional help. I'm sure I don't need to remind you what happens when we assume. For example, there is a big difference in clicking the like button on social media and recognizing the difference in a credible source online. Both of which are addressed in this book.

Overlooking communication with parents regarding a school's or teacher's digital transition is not intentional, by any stretch of the imagination. By the time educators manage all the tasks for the day, they are exhausted. Their energy has been spent playing the role of teacher, nurse, mom, dad, grandparent, cook, babysitter, administrator, fashion police, disciplinarian, friend, counselor, coach, secretary. In truth, teachers are entitled to forget a few things.

A DAY IN THE LIFE OF A LEADER IN DIGITAL EDUCATION

Just recently, I sat down in the dentist's chair, and the hygienist asked me what I did for work. When I explained that I worked in online and blended education, she looked at me with a very confused expression. In order to better explain, I followed up by asking if her child attended a school with textbooks. Not only did she understand my question (how DO they understand you when their hands are in your mouth?), but she began to share her frustration and concerns with the school's program. The good news is that I didn't have to try and talk while her hands were in my mouth. She was very frustrated with the digital learning environment her daughter participated in, so she talked during most of my dental visit.

My heart broke for her and for the school. Clearly this woman wanted to help her child when she came home with math homework that was confusing, and the school wanted to provide the best educational experience possible. The mother shared with me that she even paid for online resources to help complete homework the teacher assigned. I almost fell out of the dentist's chair with frustration, anger, and sympathy. I gasped upon hearing this, and the poor lady thought she had choked me with a dental instrument. She was a single mother. What was she thinking? What was the school thinking? Had the staff not given her tools, resources, or an orientation to teach her how to help her daughter as they made a digital transition?

The answer was no. Although the school had the best of intentions, its focus had been on the hardware in the building and the teachers. They didn't focus on the parents and the transition they would need to make in order to be involved in this new educational model. In short, the school used a different strategy to teach, not just math, than the one the mother had been taught, but also a new digital model of instruction so she was afraid to help her daughter by teaching her the "old" way. Do I hear an amen? I could certainly understand her hesitation. Since her daughter didn't have a textbook, she couldn't see examples of the "new" way to learn math in order to help her. She hadn't had 7th grade math in years. As a last resort, she fell victim to a scam and paid for help online. I was outraged.

Blended and online learning are excellent ways to teach children, which clearly the school knew, but it was breaking this mother. I knew this was not the teacher's intent, but it was also killing the daughter's love for math because she too was becoming frustrated.

In thirty minutes, while instruments, gloves, and fluoride were shoved in my mouth, I was able to relieve a bit of this mother's frustration. I gave her some tips to improve her evenings and help her assist her daughter with her homework.

Why hadn't the school provided an orientation? I cannot answer this. What I do know is that educators are so busy trying to meet mandates set in place by politicians that, when combined with doing what is best for children, little time is left for teaching parents how to use digital resources. Let's face it, there really isn't funding for parent trainings. I'd encourage you to suggest that your parent teacher association or PTA take on this challenge. Perhaps some savvy parents could put such an activity together.

Meanwhile, you have taken a tremendous step in ownership and partnership for your child's digital education by continuing to read on. You will find in the following pages, tools, and tips you can use to help your child be successful within blended and online learning environments.

Over the next several pages I will attempt to provide busy parents with tools to support your children and teachers as these new approaches for teaching are sweeping across classrooms. My goal is to provide you with a user-friendly, hands-on guide to understanding online and blended learning as well as provide you with resources to better support your child's digital education experience. The most common questions I get from parents about digital education are listed below. I have organized this book around them.

COMMON PARENT QUESTIONS ABOUT DIGITAL EDUCATION

- What on earth does all this mean? Blended, Flipped, Online, Synchronous, Asynchronous... I did well to pass Spanish, much less technical education jargon.

- I sure didn't learn this way. How do we expect children to learn with no books?

- How do I help my child if there is no textbook? They teach math differently now than when I learned it, and without a textbook I have no examples. Without examples how do I remember the correct order of operations?

- Do I pay for websites that say they will give my child examples? What do I Google?

- Hello. Is there really a teacher in there? Are they replacing teachers with computers?

- Why is my daughter failing her course? I know she was online half the night! In this environment you can demystify and prevent the shocking, failing grade.

- What is in place to make sure my child's safety is protected if he is online so much?

- What about reading? Won't my child miss out by not reading real books she can touch and smell?

- Why are schools shifting towards teaching this way, and is it really better?

- How do I work with the teacher to support my child?

- What if I don't agree? Do I have a choice in allowing my child to be educated this way?

CHAPTER 2
LET'S ATTACK THE BEAST HEAD ON: HOMEWORK...WHY?

As you read this chapter, I'd like for you to keep the homework scenario we discussed in Chapter 1 in mind. Remember, the new math, where there wasn't a textbook or worksheets? The resources for the student and mom came from websites. You may have encountered a similar scenario in your home. I have, and we will revisit this example a few times as I touch on a few topics that relate to it. In the example, I am combining homework and digital devices.

Homework online doesn't seem trivial, especially not to anyone who will be reading this. After all, you know your child is much more motivated to do homework online than a traditional worksheet. It is way cooler. From an educator's perspective, there are many more resources online to select from, kids are more engaged, and students can get immediate feedback with individualized coaching online. Let's dissect why teachers assign homework to begin with, so you know the value. While doing so, keep in mind how the transition from paper-based homework to digital homework is made more complex when you factor in your child's brain development.

A child's brain continues to develop into his mid-late 20's. Children really are not miniature adults, even if they think so. The prefrontal cortex develops last. This part of the brain is in charge of impulse control. Explains a lot, doesn't it? Pair this relatively new finding with another part of the brain that is completely developed by the teenage years, the nucleus accumbens, which is in charge of seeking pleasure and rewards (Jenson & Nutt, 2016). If the young man in the homework example had actual worksheets and a textbook, then this fancy brain talk wouldn't really matter. However, now that his homework is on a digital device and connected online, it is critical that educators, parents, and students are aware that students are hardwired during the teen years to seek pleasure and rewards, yet they don't have full impulse control. This is like sending someone with a sweet tooth, who is on a low carb diet, to a bakery to pick up cupcakes. Knowledge is power, and with the right parental engagement and support, digital homework can be much more effective than traditional worksheets.

WHY ASSIGN HOMEWORK?

Have you ever wondered why teachers actually assign homework, or if we are all just conditioned to accept it as part of a normal education? Some theories hold that teachers are trying to punish parents to make up for the suffering they endure during the day by spending 7.5 hours or so with their children. Thus, they assign loads of grueling homework. Of course, I'm kidding, but *are* teachers really trying to make parents' lives miserable by making us hold our children's feet to the fire to get them to complete their homework?

To find out the answer to that, we have to back up a century. Homework really wasn't common until the 20th century when the brain was considered a muscle that needed to be exercised like other muscles (Cooper, 2001). You might recollect seeing commercials for products that exercise your brain. That being said, the old saying, "practice makes perfect" is definitely at play when it comes to homework. In theory, if students engage and continue working the muscle, they will master concepts and fine tune the brain (Carr, 2011).

Social shifts in culture have caused the philosophy on homework to swing back and forth like a pendulum throughout the 20th and early 21st centuries. Much of this has been driven by the higher expectations of students to compete in a global market place. Preparing students for this same global market place is what is driving educators to teach using blended and online learning platforms.

One form of blended instruction (a type of digital teaching) is actually called the flipped classroom. Students do their homework during the day. Educators haven't lost their minds, but it does sound backward from the way we learned. Classroom time is literally flipped around, so understanding the purpose of homework serves many purposes as we progress. We will come back to a more in-depth definition of the flipped classroom later. For now, let's rewind and walk through some Presidential mandates over the years…

Politics has certainly influenced educational pressures. When politicians compared US students with international populations and felt pressures that we were being outpaced based on data presented in the publication of A Nation at Risk (1983) expectations for the American education system increased. Suddenly more was expected of children (United States National Commission on Excellence in Education). Additionally, added pressures on educators around increased standards stemmed from No Child Left Behind (2002). Suddenly teachers were expected to have 100% of students passing/graduating. Teachers didn't receive additional classroom support, and the traditional classroom structures didn't change, for the most part. However, the expectations on teachers and students certainly did, as did the accountability system to measure whether or not teachers were effectively accomplishing these goals. The result? Teachers began cramming in as much information as they could, and that meant more homework because there are only so many hours in a school day. Fast forward to the implementation of Common Core Standards (or whatever name your state is using for their version of the Common Core standards). This is a different approach to thinking that requires rigor and for students to be able to relate academic content to the real-world. They need to be able to think critically. Today, we find ourselves living in a homework crazed period just so teachers and students can meet minimum requirements to pass state tests.

In other words, teachers tend to assign homework for two reasons:

1. They believe that students need to practice what they learn, and they simply run out of time in class.

Using classroom time to work with students and having them do independent work at home provides an opportunity for students to practice, allowing them to master new concepts. I'd compare this to doing bicep curls. If you do high reps with low to medium weight you will see muscle definition. This homework process will give your child academic "muscle definition" and also allows teachers to teach concepts during class. Assigning homework allows teachers more time in class to cover new standards or allows them to cover more material.

2. Some teachers feel like they need to give students more practice (bicep curls) to prepare them for current testing practices or requirements, while others feel like less is more (think low reps, high weight), shifting the focus to quality over quantity.

Teachers who believe *less is more* often assign more project-based activities. These activities usually resemble what you'd see in a workplace to complete a project or task and they involve students working together to create a product. Most of us accept homework as a norm in our culture because we (and our parents) had homework in school. But, now our children come home with homework that mainly requires technology instead of textbooks like we or our parents had. *Why?*

There is a great answer to this question. As you know, technology engages children. This is often why the best punishment for our children is to take away their devices. Similarly, it motivates them to complete their school work. The American Institute for Research (2002) found that students who used the internet to complete their homework finished it more quickly than those who did not. That was over 16 years ago. Think of the developments in social media alone over the last decade. Can you imagine the impact technological advancements have had on how our school-age children complete their homework now? Do you imagine the internet sites started during the last year possess more valuable resources than those sites we might have found in 2002? Of course they do, and this is another reason to assign children homework online.

We are discovering more advances in technology; teachers are learning better ways to teach with it; and students are growing up in a digital world. It only seems logical that they complete homework faster when they have immediate access to information, and they are able to access that information in a manner in which they are comfortable and knowledgeable (Levin & Arafeh, 2002).

I don't think this next fact will surprise you either. When students were given the option of participating in a discussion face-to-face or online in a discussion forum, the online discussion forum had much higher quality responses from the students than the classroom discussion (Grisham & Wolsey, 2006).

Why is this the case? You know your child, so let's explore this study a bit and put it into perspective. Actually, first go back to your high school days. Imagine it is 4th period, and you had gym 3rd period. You know where I'm going. You are self-conscious because you are all sweaty, and, of course, you had a crush on the kid a row over (within smelling distance). Now, the teacher isn't all that sensitive to the fact that you are a bit nervous already. Who wouldn't be, given the circumstances?

Today's assignment? An in-class discussion. You are asked to "Compare the tactics of the rebels during The Cold War and the rebels in present day Syria". You haven't the faintest clue how to answer the question and sound intelligent, and...*Oh my...your high school crush looks your way. Oh my...is that a zit on your chin? Oh Geez...You better not draw any undue attention to yourself.*

You can imagine, then, that, in front of the class, as you respond with all the social pressure, you may not give as high of a quality response as you would if you were online. Not to mention that you do not have "Google" at your fingertips to research the answer.

In an online discussion forum, you don't have to worry so much about "sounding dumb" and embarrassing yourself in front of the big crush a few seats over. Additionally, you have the chance to take advantage of the quick research tool with which you are most accustomed, Google. You have time to think through and create a response in writing, edit it, and run spell check; all before jumping into the discussion.

From that perspective, it is a no brainer that online discussion forums have higher quality responses than in-class discussions. An additional component to consider is that all students get the chance to participate in an online discussion, not just the ones who are quick on their feet, the closest to the teacher, or the loudest. This means that the teacher can interact with ALL students in the class and evaluate each student's level of understanding, which allows the teacher to personalize future work.

Surely this is just a trend, though. Why would students all across the world suddenly be more motivated to do their homework just because technology is included? Let's jump back into your high school history class, and I promise this time it won't be as painful as the experience I just described…no pimples, no sweat, and definitely no essays required.

Premodern times were governed by traditional beliefs and religion, but modern times looked towards science and reason to answer questions and provide guidance toward social enlightenment. What does that mean? History supports what we have learned as parents. When you encourage one thing, people do the opposite. You have experienced this with your children, right? As soon as you say, "No" they seem to be more attracted to desire the forbidden fruit. Premodern times ended in about 1973, which brings us to the postmodern era, a time that is unlike previous eras, mainly because of the influence of computers and the internet on the way we live and work.

Still in history class—Let's look at some influential changes to the postmodern era that have shaped our culture. The first computer was used for instruction in the 1950s, but it was physically HUGE (Roblyer & Doering, 2013). However, in the mid-1970s we had the introduction of the micro-computer (one that didn't take up an entire room). Combine this with the fact that a project by the U.S. Department of Defense, ARPAnet (the foundation of the internet) began in the early 1970's, and you have a recipe for building a great cultural shift and the foundation for a very tech savvy generation to emerge (Oliver, 2013; Roblyer & Doering, 2013).

Okay, the history lesson is over. You know the rest because you are living it, which makes YOU the expert. This is exactly why you WILL be able to help your child with digital homework after you read this book.

EDUTAINMENT

"When my son asked for a tablet for Christmas, I thought he just wanted to play games!"

Exactly. You are correct. You have to give educators credit. They can be pretty smart cookies. Why not teach kids in a way they like to play and be entertained? Shouldn't that be a great way to engage them? After all, this is the postmodern era, one where our children have been taught that education should be entertaining.

Who doesn't love something red and furry that giggles (Elmo) or talking teddy bears that play educational games? Did you see that Teddy Ruxpin came back in 2017, except instead of a cassette tape, he has LCD eyes and an app! Does it get any better?! These are examples of "edutainment" at the earliest stages. C'mon. How are teachers supposed to compete with Sesame Street?

Here are some amazing statistics about youngsters and their exposure to technology as edutainment.

- 90% of parents with children under age two let their kids use electronic media (Braiker, 2013).

- In 2011, 52% of homes with children ages eight and younger had access to a mobile device. In 2017, 98% had access to a mobile device (Rideout, 2017).

- In 2011, 4% of screen time for children eight and under was mobile, but in 2017 mobile screen time increased to 35% for children under age eight (Rideout, 2017).

- Since 2013, the amount of time young children spend on mobile devices has tripled from 15 minutes a day to 48 minutes a day in 2017 (Rideout, 2017).

- More than ¼ of parents have downloaded apps for their children (Rideout, 2011).

- 72% of iTunes top selling apps are designed for preschoolers and elementary children (Shuler, 2012)

- In 2017, an average 21-year-old had consumed: 5,000 hours playing video games; 250,000 emails, instant messages, and/or texts; 10,000 hours of cell phone use, and 3500 hours online (Weinberger, 2017).

So, now that you need to pick your jaw up off the floor or are nodding your head in agreement, here is what we know about kids today. You know this because you are a parent, grandparent, guardian, aunt, or uncle of a school age child. Otherwise you wouldn't be reading this book. Children are ALWAYS connected, but remember if they are teenagers, their brains are fully developed to seek pleasure and rewards, just not impulse control. So, even though their digital devices are basically an additional appendage, they still need you.

Let's dig into a bit more research, though, as we unpack how we got here. While most of you are either Generation X (with birthdates in the 1960s - early 1980s) or Generation Y/Millennials (with birthdates in the 1980s-early 2000s), your children, grandchildren, or dependents are either part of the Generation Y/Millennial generation or they are in Generation Z. You may have also heard this generation referred to as the Net Generation. Generation Z, specifically, includes "kids" as I call them, who are born in the late 1990s or mid 2000's. This is where I will spend most of my focus since the NeXters from Gen Z are the ones you are currently parenting, as am I.

This generation (Z), in contrast to previous generations, has been connected since an early age, as evidenced by my previous edutainment examples. Another way to think of the differentiation in Gen Z from other generations is by considering some hard-parenting decisions you have had to make in comparison to those your parents had to make. Did your parents have to decide at what age it was appropriate to let you have a cell phone? I'd say, probably not, at least not when you were in elementary or middle school, for sure. However, I am certain you have either purchased or considered purchasing a smart device for your child. Depending on the age of the Gen Z child you were thinking of when you purchased this book, I can surmise that you have had conversations with other parents on the birthday circuit about at what age you will consider purchasing a smart device for your oldest.

The intentions or considerations to purchase a smart device for your Gen Z dependent are or were most likely for security and convenience. I'm sure your Gen Z dependent has or will find many other applications for the device(s). Case in point, in 2017, the average American teenager was sending 3300 text messages monthly (Nielson, 2018). Gen Z has experienced a lifetime of immediate communication and information; therefore, its members expect instant access and resources. They are often referred to as "digital natives" because of this. They are very familiar with instant messaging, text messaging, email, smart phones, RSS feeds, tweets, and social media, but you don't likely need me to tell YOU this.

Of course, some research says that so much interaction with technology actually changes the way kids think. Literally, there is theory that constant exposure to technology changes the physical structure of the brain. One area I will explore is literacy and how our children are reading differently than previous generations. The American Academy of Pediatrics (AAP) states that children under the age of two receive no benefits from any digital device (television, gaming, educational games…), and that over the age of 2, children need no more than 2 hours of entertainment per day (Ghose, 2016). Time is better spent socializing and being active. On average, 8-year-olds spend 8 hours a day using some form of media. Teenagers, though, spend more than 11 hours a day. In 2013 teenagers spent an average of 3,600 texts per month, according to Common Sense Media (2017), and girls send more texts than do boys (Rideout & Robb, 2018).

Since children and teenagers are using digital devices in school and at home. It is important to maintain a holistic view of their screen time (Some tools to help monitor screen time are: MomentFamily, UnGlue, Bark, Circle by Disney, to name a few). Screen time adds up very quickly, as you read in Chapter One. The American Association of Pediatrics provides extremely helpful guidelines. For example, when my daughter was in kindergarten, she watched a movie at school before holiday break which fulfilled her recommended hour (and then some) for the day of media consumption. That meant no screen time at home that evening.

AMERICAN ACADEMY OF PEDIATRIC'S (AAP) RECOMMENDED SCREEN TIME

AGE	AAP'S RECOMMENDATIONS
< 18 months	Avoid screen time except for video chatting, if you wish.
18-24 months	If you want to introduce digital media, choose high-quality programming, and explain it as your child watches.
2-5 years	Limit digital media to one hour per day. Choose high-quality programming and explain it as your child watches by applying it to the world around him.
6 years and older	Place time limits on the use of media and the types of media. Make sure the media doesn't interfere with adequate sleep, physical activity, or other essential activities.

Designate media free times such as dinner or driving, and have media-free rooms, such as bedrooms.

Have ongoing conversations about online citizenship and safety, including treating others with respect offline and online. |

A "Family Media Use Tool" provided by AAP that may be helpful for you, can be found at www.HealthyChildren.org/MediciaUsePlan.

It doesn't take a rocket scientist to figure out that if children sit and play a gaming device or watch television for 5 hours a day instead of playing outside or interacting with adults or other children they are missing out on crucial development skills such as socialization or exercise. A study out of the UK showed the extreme side of what happens when infants are over-exposed to digital devices. The use of household tablets doubled in 2013 from 20 to 51%, which is impacting children's social and physical development. A teacher from Northern Ireland shared that his colleagues "talk of pupils who come into their classrooms after spending most of the previous night playing computer games and whose attention span is so limited that they may as well not be there" (Paton 2014, p. 1).

He went on to explain that he had spoken with daycare teachers, where children could swipe a screen but didn't have the motor skills to stack blocks (Paton, 2014). I know you have been in restaurants where parents quiet toddlers by handing them gaming devices or mobile devices rather than interacting with them or allowing them to play with crayons. Unless the child has a sensory challenge, where the screen time is a therapy, this is a great temporary fix, but what does this do long term? In other words, there are wonderful benefits to infusing technology and digital devices into our society and education system, but there is also a balance that must be achieved. At home, parents must be conscientious and aware, to assure the safety and development of the whole child.

Our brains, and especially those of our kids, process information that we read online differently than information we read in textbooks. This is one reason why national education standards now include technical literacy standards. For example, students in the Net Generation have trained their brains to read by skipping around on websites, scanning for pertinent information. Science even suggests that their brains are being wired differently. Whereas older generations are more likely to read from left to right and top to bottom as a result of our training and exposure to paper-based materials. Think of the differences in motor skills it takes to scroll down a page and slide it around on the screen as opposed to turning a paper page when reading a book. Can you imagine how these actions would engage the brain differently?

GENERATION Z

Remember that your child is always connected. Of the 95% of children in the US who have smartphones, 45% of them say they are constantly connected (Anderson & Jiang, 2018). Access to a wealth of resources and information leads to a culture of instant information and speed. Consider how much information is on a webpage. There could be, video, audio, navigation tools, widgets with RSS feeds and/or advertisements, etc. Generation Z readers scan pages for the information they need and move to another website or resource if they do not find that information quickly by glancing at headlines or headers (Carr, 2011). This should also explain why researchers at American Institute of Research (2002) found that children who use the internet complete their homework quicker than those who do not (Levin & Arafeh, 2002). Of course, they do.

So, it makes sense that Generation Z learns better in the school day and with homework by integrating technology. We had Encyclopedia Britannicas, so we learned better with paper. Gen Z has never even answered the door when an encyclopedia salesman rang the doorbell. They wouldn't even understand a joke about it. If they are always connected to technology in their social lives it makes sense that they are motivated in a learning environment where they are more comfortable and engaged.

I've included a quick reference list of facts about Generation Z that might interest you.

- Children in Gen Z have immediate access to publishing their thoughts and ideas through social media such as Twitter, Facebook, blogs and YouTube.
- They are master multi-taskers since they multi-task nonstop.
- They must be taught to be creative.
- 64% have constant internet access.

- They spend eight to nine hours per day connected to at least one form of media.

- 90% of secondary students have mobile devices.

- 20% of elementary students have mobile devices.

- They are the most independent generation because they have had less direct parent supervision since they have usually been in daycare as a result of being in single parent homes or having mothers in the workforce.

- Gen Z spends less time than any others in human history using conversation to communicate.

- They view marriage as less important, but they view parenting as much more important.

- They have more purchasing power than any previous generation did at a comparable age.

- They have higher rates of obesity.

- They are extremely social and group oriented.

- They are diverse and tolerant of diversity.

- They prefer game-like learning situations.

- They are more visual than other generations.

- Bad news—They live at home longer than any previous generations!

- Obviously, they utilize technology more than other previous generations.

- They view technology as a given, not a reward or piece of equipment. It is a necessity.

- They place value on the speed of their work, not accuracy.

- Their attention span is shorter, and they have a high dependency on technology.

(Elmore, 2012; Fedock & Young, 2013; Kemp, n.d.; Kinash, Wood, & Knight, 2013; Kotchick, & Forehand, 2002; Miller, 2011; Rozario, 2011; Schroer, 2004; Taylor, 2004; Dolot, 2018)

There is a mass entrance of mothers into the workforce when compared to previous generations, and the high divorce rate has created more dual career and single parent families (Taylor, 2004). Don't let this make you feel guilty because, even though you are working and being a parent, you are the most involved parents of any generation. Generation Z is also known for being more sheltered than other children of a comparable age in previous generations. For example, Generation Z is more involved in recreational events than any previous generation. They are also extremely focused on grades and performance (Taylor, 2004). How do you pull this all off of as busy, working parents? Let me add that oftentimes you are referred to as helicopter parents, meaning you swoop in and save the day...constantly. I include myself in this category.

So, we see a new shift in education that forces us, as parents and educators, to structure time management more wisely. We do this while we meet the needs of a very different postmodern era than we have traditionally faced in education. The drive to implement technology can help us face these challenges if we know how to use the technology while we view it as a resource rather than a problem or distraction. By the way, this is exactly how we want our children to be prepared…to use technology in the global workforce.

STUDENT STORY

When Eugenia was adopted she had to learn English as her second language, and she was hearing impaired in one ear. By the time she was in high school, she was really self-conscious regarding her hearing challenge. Even though she was raised in the US, she had to work harder than her peers in order to read and understand literature since English was not her native language. Her mother decided to enroll her in an online English class. For the first time, Eugenia earned an A in English! She could read and re-read the curriculum at her own pace. She didn't have to raise her hand in front of the class to ask the teacher to repeat instruction. Her confidence soared, and her language skills improved drastically.

CHAPTER 3
HAS MY CHILD'S TEACHER FLIPPED? NO PAPER?

EVERYONE IS AN EXPERT

Every generation has had defining moments happen when they are students. One defining moment during my elementary school experience was in 1986 when the Space Shuttle Challenger exploded. I was in 2nd grade. We were all gathered in Mrs. Blue's classroom watching a portable television. I will never forget it.

Similarly, as a teacher, I will never forget the group of students with whom I gathered in the lobby of the small Christian school, where I taught on September 11, 2001. I still feel the somberness and shock of raw emotion as we prayed while CNN replayed the crash into the twin towers over and over.

After the Russians launched Sputnik in 1957, duck and cover drills became the norm as students were trained to prepare for a nuclear attack from Russia. My parents, of course, remember the Cuban Missile Crisis, which also spurred more drills in schools in fear of attack.

Besides the horrific life-changing events such as the ones I just described, there were daily operations I never even noticed, which impacted my education. Ironically, these norms are just as embedded in my memory bank as the others, and they are equally as driven by technology. What I didn't realize was that these day-to-day activities, such as using an overhead projector, would soon be obsolete, and the classroom of yesterday would in no way look like it does today.

Because everyone shares similar memories of their schooling, be it the memories I described or different ones, and we all experienced them for approximately thirteen years, education is the one profession where, regardless of training, everyone has experienced it. Everyone having an opinion isn't always a good thing, which is why we see education criticized all the time. For example, how often do you hear people criticizing the way a surgeon runs his or her operating room? That is what I thought. Why is everyone an "expert"? It is because we all went to school, of course. We all have memories of great teachers and lessons or activities we really liked and learned during. It is also because education is one of the fields in which the majority of people have a vested interest. Why? Because they have children.

Remember the activities or lessons that you loved in school? At the core, good instruction is still *good instruction*. Nobody will argue that. The main difference is that we have new tools and new ways to engage students, which are necessary because the way to engage this generation is different than the previous generations. Ideally, we teach them in the way that they like to play. I know what you are thinking. "No way, I had to walk five miles in the snow to school one way. Now you want my child to learn doing something called edutainment?"

First of all, your great grandparents were the ones who walked five miles in the snow. I get it. They were barefoot, but as Bob Dylan said, "These Times They Are a-Changin." I refer you back to the Generation Z descriptors in Chapter Two. Generation Z is used to being entertained, and 90% of parents with children under 2 let their children use electronic media. That is peak time in the brain's development (Braiker, 2013; Roizen & Oz, 2010). I'm not saying this is the best thing to do for a baby's brain, but it is what it is.

All of this means that your children are wired differently than you are, so they learn differently. It is okay to admit that you hand or handed your child your smart phone to play a game when you needed five minutes of peace and quiet. Remember, this is also the generation with the highest number of single parents. Trust me. I can relate. Moderation and balance are key when it comes to letting children play on digital devices.

Children seek edutainment because their brains have been trained differently as a result of the great increase in technology exposure. Everything reacts, flashes, and talks. This exposure has caused developmental skills to change drastically. Members of the Association of Teachers and Lecturers (2014) found that some infants don't have the motor skills needed to play with building blocks because they are playing with tablet computers and smartphones instead. Ownership of computer tablets in homes more than doubled in one year, from 20% in 2013 to 51% in 2014. The next time you go to a restaurant notice why all the toddlers are so well behaved. They are all playing on Mommy or Daddy's phone instead of throwing crayons. With moderation, edutainment is not a bad thing. There are specific vision disorders with apps to train the muscles of the eyes for better coordination in young toddlers, for example, and educational apps represent the second highest category in App Store sales with 72% of the top-selling education apps designated for preschoolers through early grade schoolers (Schuler, 2012).

An easy example of edutainment that you might relate to is *Sesame Street*. Mine Craft, however, is not edutainment. It is simply a game for entertainment. That is not to suggest, though, that games cannot be educational. A great way for students to learn is through game-based learning, which is a form of edutainment. Remember that in 2017, 80,000 apps in the app store were categorized as education, but who tested them to see if they were effective learning tools? Errrr...My suggestion? Common Sense Media, www.commonsensemedia.com, has loads of tools to help you with how to select resources and provides research and guidance for the digital era. I highly recommend you check it out!

Think back to your favorite teacher. Chances are it was probably someone who was funny or warm. Maybe the teacher did fun activities or experiments? This is what we typically hear when we ask someone about his or her favorite teacher. Thanks to the infusion of technology, digital content allows all teachers to be fun if they know how to integrate it correctly. This makes going to school a lot better for most kids.

You probably watched movies in school, but I bet you weren't allowed to have your cell phone in class, if you had one. Your parents, on the other hand, definitely didn't have a cell phone in class, and I bet they can remember watching films and movies. Education adjusts to meet the learning needs of every generation. The technology of Generation

Z, however; is drastically shaping our culture in such a way that it is reshaping education, the workforce, and our own cultural expectations. Thus, the classroom of tomorrow will look very different than even the classroom of today. Regardless of whether your technique is edutainment, educational technology does help prepare children for the workforce, one that is losing 10,000 Baby Boomers a day to retirement, only to find that half of the workforce does not have the skills to replace them (Echols, 2014; Organization for Economic Cooperation and Development, 2012). It is important to teach children technical skills.

Let's look at something that might look painfully familiar to all generations.

$$a^2+b^2=c^2$$

Urggg…. I get nauseous even thinking of the Pythagorean Theorem. I brought my teacher, Mrs. Dickson, homemade biscuits so she'd work through her lunch and tutor me— no joke. I made it through it, and I survived Triangle Inequalities but not without pain. Is any of this ringing a bell or causing anxiety? Because my teacher had strong pedagogy, the knowledge of good instructional skills, or by the grace of God combined with sheer will, I made it through all of the miserable theorems in a traditional classroom.

EXPERIENTIAL LEARNING WITH TECHNOLOGY

Wouldn't you have rather manipulated 3D objects and seen the real-world application of Geometry than stayed in your desk with your protractor where you asked, "When am I ever going to need to know these theorems in real life?" Well, the modern classroom brings in those experiential opportunities. By integrating technology, students have a simulated learning experience where they decide what size television to buy. Using the Pythagorean theorem, they decide on the diagonal size of the television once given the space on the wall to fill. Through experiential opportunities they try multiple sized televisions to see which one fits using a handheld device. This allows them to actually slide televisions around on the wall space on the screen. This is a very different type of multiple-choice test than you or I has taken, and you cannot do this with real televisions unless your child's school has a budget unlike any school I've ever been in. This simulation might also include budgeting experience, something with which all American students need to practice.

Other experiential ways to apply the theorem could include assuming the role of a carpenter and cutting carpet for a room. With this experience, students virtually cut the carpet based on their problem solving and try out multiple measurements without actually ever cutting a piece of carpet or messing up your living room. In this example, the teacher has the choice whether to ask students to spend all their class time cutting pieces of real carpet that have been donated, or spend 10 minutes completing the same task in an online simulation. The second choice gives them the opportunity to then move on to more learning. Do you remember what we discussed in Chapter One? Your children are part of Generation Z. Their attention span is different than yours. They are engaged by activities that include technology, and they need to learn to apply technology with problem-solving skills in order to be prepared for the 21st century job market.

Now, do you really think your children want to physically cut up pieces of carpet to learn the Pythagorean Theorem or that they want to draw triangles on paper? Nope. They want to manipulate objects on handheld devices, where there is no fear of failure because they can just wipe the slate clean and try again. Wouldn't you?

Obviously, there needs to be a balance. The benefits of technology do not justify giving in to allow your child to be connected 24/7. As a matter of fact, I agree with educators who are begging parents to create a balance at home. I will discuss tips and strategies for balancing screen time in Chapter 4. Teachers find it difficult to manage children who have developed shorter attention spans because they are used to being entertained by animated games. These expectations are not aligned to real life, and they create a difficult transition for education and also for socialization.

It is fantastic to be proud that your child can operate your mobile device at age two, but he should also be responding to his own name by then and making eye contact. At home, just like in the classroom, technology should be used as a tool for engagement and opportunity.

Let's revisit that surgeon I mentioned a little while ago. Would you request a surgeon that refused to use technology during procedures? That is not a trick question. I believe the answer to the question is a resounding, "NO." I sure hope it is. That being said, think about how common technology is in the workplace. What if you couldn't use Google hangouts, Skype, Adobe Connect or a similar service for your remote meetings or teleconferences? These examples are part of the norms of our everyday lives. So why wouldn't we implement the same technologies in our schools since our children will be expected to know them when they are in the workforce? I don't necessarily have an answer to that question, but change is hard for all of us whether we are teachers, students, or parents. When you begin to get frustrated with the process of learning a new way of helping your child(ren), remember what life would be like if we didn't integrate technology into our own daily lives. I think we all choose the "blended surgery center" over the "traditional surgery center" any day!

You may still feel that this all sounds great in theory but have no idea what how your child is really doing at school. I hear all kinds of comments:

- *All I know is my daughter came home with an assignment to look something up on the internet.*

- *My son doesn't have a math textbook. Instead he has worksheets, and I have no idea how to do this kind of division.*

- *Supposedly the answers are online somewhere?*

If this sounds like you, you are not alone. Let's investigate the types of digital classrooms your child or children may experience.

TYPES OF DIGITAL CLASSROOMS

Students can be taught in a digital classroom in a variety of ways. The hardware, physical set up, or style of the classroom is impacted by the instructional model for the digital resources. Each teacher may be at a different level of comfort or implementation with the digital resources or curriculum, which also impacts the instructional model. All of these factors affect how you are able to support your child's learning experience. However, if you understand the basic idea behind the model the teacher is using you will be better equipped to support both your child and the teacher.

The Blended Classroom

In the blended classroom the teacher "blends" traditional teaching, like we had in school, with other strategies that include technology. The teacher may have the students rotate in stations to engage in different assignments, a lot like you might remember from elementary school. At least one of the stations involves technology, and the teacher becomes a facilitator by integrating technology into the blended environment. Instead of standing in front of your child and lecturing, ideally, the teacher helps as each student progresses through the assignments. This is called the "Station Rotation Model." A similar approach could be done if students go to a computer lab to work on specific assignments for a subject, and this is called a "Lab Rotation" model (Horn & Staker, 2014, pp. 39-41).

Components of each lesson may still be delivered traditionally, and there is nothing wrong with this. However, certain components of the lesson (or whole lessons at times) may be better delivered through the use of technology. The blended classroom takes advantage of the best of both worlds; the traditional and the online mediums. Blended classrooms allow teachers to individualize learning.

One significant positive to this model is that it is possible and often likely that students have a personalized learning plan. Just like in the 1:1 model, it is important to remember that the level of implementation of this model varies significantly depending on the teachers' comfort with technology, training, experience, and the software provided.

Also, be cautious to remember that just because a teacher assigns students to look up something on the internet and print it off, this does not mean your child is in a blended classroom. This is simply called using the internet. It isn't much different than standing at a copying machine making a photocopy. In other words, a blended classroom uses the technology as an instructional tool, not merely a resource for information. There are varieties within the different models of blended instruction. All models, though, include an online component and a face-to-face component. Interaction with and facilitation by a talented educator is critical for success in this model.

The 1:1 Classroom

In this classroom, the 1:1 refers to assigning 1 device to 1 student. In such settings the device can be a tablet, computer, or other mobile device. The teacher usually serves as a facilitator, not as the "sage on the stage," like in a traditional classroom. You will not see the teacher write on the board and do all the talking. Access to this type of technology allows the teacher to engage your child in activities that are aligned to his or her individual needs. In a traditional classroom, the teacher may have up to 35 students, where he or she is required to meet everyone's needs at the same time. In this traditional scenario, the teacher may also choose to teach to the top of the class (higher achieving students) or the middle (average skill level). This choice often depends on how many students fall into each group of academic ability. This can be very hard, and as you can imagine, some children get left behind while others get bored.

Experienced teachers may implement what is called "differentiated instruction" to try and meet individual children's needs. Each student receives a different assignment based on the child's strengths and/or skills. This requires a lot of advanced preparation by the teacher. In a classroom with advanced technology, the teacher can implement individualized instruction for each student with less planning and preparation because the software is often responsive or adaptive to students' specific needs. It is a lot like Amazon, Netflix, or Google. Have you noticed how these algorithms get more and more accurate each time you use them at recommending what you might like? Their recommendation engines use your previous choices to suggest what you might like. Over time, they gather more and more data, which allows them to become more accurate, much like the same adaptive software in education.

There is educational software smart enough to measure whether your child needs more practice or if he or she can move on. One student may need five practice activities to master a concept, while another may only need two. The technology can also tell if your child needs to practice a skill he or she may not have mastered last year. The software may analyze how your child learns best. The type of blended learning model I've described here is an "Individualized Rotation" because the students work on their own devices, and the software is based on their individualized needs (Horn & Staker, 2014, pp. 45-46).

It is important to remember that the level of implementation of the 1:1 model significantly depends on the teachers' comfort with technology, training, experience, and the software provided. A 1:1 initiative may look very different in classrooms throughout a school or it may be just one component of activities in a teacher's classroom.

FROM WHERE DO THE DEVICES COME? WHO IS RESPONSIBLE?

Lab

This model is straight forward and the easiest to implement. When your child gets to school, he picks up a laptop from the mobile cart in his classroom and takes it to his desk, or he may sit at a particular computer station in a computer lab. Both you and your child should be asked to review and agree to the school's Acceptable Use Policy (AUP), at minimum, which defines the expectations, policies, and procedures for digital citizenship when using school property. See Appendix B for an example from Boston Public Schools. According to the Consortium for School Networking (CoSN), the school's AUP should include definitions, acceptable uses, unacceptable uses, policy statement, and violations/sanctions. It should also outline the consequences if your child violates any of the school policies or procedures. Your child's school, under USDOE's Keeping Children Safe in Education Policy (2018), should have safeguards in place such as effective web filtering, online safety information, and e-safety policies.

In this situation it is critical to discuss with your child the importance of not sharing any passwords or even logging into any accounts on the school machine that you may allow him to log into at home. If your child goes to school on a half day before a break, for example, where the teachers tells them they can play on the computers, and let's say your savvy 9th grader or even your 2nd grader, for that matter, decides to enter his Netflix user ID and PW to watch a movie. It is very likely that the next student coming in could log into your account just by accident. It is critical to discuss that computers have "memories" when it comes to passwords. See Appendix A for steps on how to delete passwords on public computers.

BYOD (Bring Your Own Device)

This sounds like a term we used to refer to parties when I was in college. If you agree, well, you are pretty close. This term actually stands for, "Bring Your Own Device," and the device can be anything from a tablet to a mobile device. For a BYOD classroom, students are required to bring their own devices to school in order to log into the schools WIFI rather than relying on the school to provide devices.

There are some considerations you may want to investigate if your child is part of a BYOD school system. First, be sure to read the schools Acceptable Use Policy (AUP). This is the policy outlining the rules and expectations you must agree to in order for your child to access the school or school district internet and to take advantage of their technology resources. Technically, you should be signing the AUP each year, as should your child.

Second, if your child is in a BYOD situation, you will want to consider internet history and sites your child uses for school on the computer, especially if you use the computer for other purposes such as online purchases or social media. If your child takes a device to school that you have used to purchase something online, you are creating an opportunity for someone to gain access to: (a) your identity, (b) your purchasing information and history, (c) the location of your home, and (d) your social media history.

Why does this matter? Nothing is free. Let's use Facebook as an example. Sure, we don't pay anything out of our pockets to look at our pictures of our friend's new baby, but we are giving advertisers data as our currency. How's that? Our data, in the form of views and likes, are equivalent to money for advertisers. Similarly, many of the "free" educational resource sites have usage terms buried or hidden in their privacy policies stating that they aren't responsible for how their third-party partners use data collected from cookies on your device once your child creates a user account. You, of course, have to agree to the user account, but I have seen MANY teachers ask students to create accounts without realizing that there is a requirement for parental permission and/or this kind of data is collected. Certainly, they don't know it is shared with third parties. Free is never really free, and most teachers have not been sufficiently trained in online resources.

We have to be equally as knowledgeable and involved when it comes to our children's or, in this case, our, personally identifiable information. I have provided step-by-step instructions for you on how to clear your internet history in Appendix C.

In Chapter 4, I go into detail about popular educational sites and what to consider when you are looking for ones that are both reputable and free.

TAKING HOME A DEVICE

Now, let's imagine the situation is the opposite, and your child brings home a device from school. This happens in a lot in second grade and older classes. There are some things you will want to review in the AUP. Which sites are restricted? Can your child log in on your wireless internet at home and bypass the school's security protection? It is unlikely, but not all school Internet Technology (IT) systems or IT Directors are alike. If there is a camera on a computer that your child brings home, is it disabled? If not, I'd suggest covering it. Actually, I suggest disabling or covering all cameras on devices in your home unless you are talking with friends or family, and the camera is in use. Why do I suggest this?

If you have a router for your wireless internet at home, then it came with a default password. Many times, people don't change the default password to a secure password—one that is private to them. Since brands of routers have common default passwords, people with malicious intentions can hack into your home network by using the default password. When they do, they can see into your home through the camera on your computer. Pretty frightening, huh? Let me put this into context. If someone was planning to commit a crime in your home, he could learn your habits and the map of your home just by logging into your network. If you haven't done so, then you need to change that password! You can also get little covers for your camera for less than $5.00, that slide right off when you want to have a video conversation for school, work, or with family.

Checking with the IT department or on the computer your child may bring home to ensure that the camera is disabled is one option to ensure your child's safety, but what if your child is in an online course or in a program where the students meet online? In this situation, you can enable the camera when needed. Other options include the webcam cover I just described, or make sure your child doesn't have the device in a bedroom or other private area. This is always the best practice. There have been situations where administrators have watched children through webcams of school issued machines, if they suspected activities with drugs, while the children were in the privacy of their homes. In this situation, the administrator had good intentions, but a line was crossed. Unfortunately, not everyone has good intentions, so I suggest that knowledge is power when it comes to privacy.

Restricting access to the camera in private settings will prevent a lot of heartache when it comes to social media and oversharing during middle school and high school, as we will discuss in Chapter 5. The sooner you implement consistency on your rules for the camera and allowing others into your home digitally, the better.

SO, HOW IS THE TEACHING DIFFERENT WITH DEVICES?

1:1

Regardless of how the students access their machines (lab, school provided 1:1, BYOD), a 1:1 model where each student has a device creates flexible opportunities for teachers to design instruction. Horn and Staker (2014) defined models for the blended classroom that many educators follow. The following explanations may be helpful to you as you identify the style of blended learning your child's teacher is using.

Individual Rotation – In this model, your child works using the device assigned to him, where he'd work through specific digital curriculum or software to meet his individual needs. This is sometimes referred to as a playlist, where the individualized curriculum is delivered to your child via the platform.

Station Rotation – In a station rotation model, students stay within their classrooms, and they rotate through different learning stations (a lot like elementary school). In at least one of those stations, students do work that is customized for their learning. Other stations may be more generalized or contain a variety of activities. Students attend all of the stations during class. This model often gives the teacher the flexibility to work with students in one of the stations.

Lab Rotation – If the 1:1 model is in a lab we call this a lab rotation. In this model of instruction, the teacher takes the students to the computer lab, where they complete their digital activities to support the lesson.

Recognizing that all of those models seem like we are fitting technology into the traditional model of education, let's discuss some creative ways educators are getting outside of the box through digital education.

The Flipped Classroom

The flipped classroom is a form of the blended classroom that requires a very dedicated student. When we were in school, we typically spent our time in the classroom learning a new skill or concept. Then we'd have classwork and then additional homework. How many times, though, did you get stuck working on the homework and wish you had your teacher there to help you? In theory, the flipped model of the blended classroom allows the students the opportunity to have hands on interactive practice during the school day with other students, mentors, teachers, or in an apprenticeship because at night they are completing what would have traditionally been called classwork. In order for this model to be successful, the teacher provides online assignments, "lectures," or teaching through videos that students must view at home the night before or during their free time. This is done beforehand so students can practice the skills taught in the online activities when they attend class.

During the school day, the student works through the activities that support the practice of learning, in class, where he or she has access to the teacher, should the student need support or help. How many of us have trouble doing 6th grade math homework? Or how many of us have begrudged a teacher for assigning a group project for homework? Yup…I'm guilty too.

The flipped classroom model allows the student to have direct access to the teacher during the time we know as homework. Technology allows this model of education to be a reality. Each student is responsible to learn the content outside of the classroom and come ready to participate in the projects or practice during the school day. Poof! No more hosting group projects at your house until 11 pm. I'm not sure it is that easy, but you get the concept.

Online Classes

The first online school started in 1996 in Massachusetts, so while still a young field, it isn't quite as new as most people think. As a matter of fact, there is quite a bit of guidance on what governs a quality online class, such as, standards in place by Quality Matters (QM), National Standards for Quality (NSQ), and Oliver's Frameworks for Online and Blended Instruction. Best practices exist that were created from teaching standards. These standards include the framework for how courses should be designed. So, if you are looking for ideas on what you should expect or something to compare your child's experience to, I suggest looking at: www.blendedpractice.com and/or www.nsqol.org.

An online or virtual class is one where the teacher and student are separate, and the course takes place over the internet. A syllabus or course outline should be available to parents for the course that explains the course requirements. A pacing guide with due dates for assignments should also be available. Usually and hopefully, there are ways for students to interact with the teacher in an online course such as chat features, email, discussion forums, and/or the teacher will have posted office hours. The teacher may even have a weekly live lesson, where the student can interact with the teacher live. The teacher usually has a calendar with due dates, so you can help your child manage his or her time and plan when to submit his or her assignments, which you need to do. One of the most challenging aspects of an online class for students is procrastination. Imagine that. Would your child procrastinate?

As a founder and administrator of both a district-wide and a state-wide online school, I consistently saw that students' greatest challenge in an online class was time management. One of the best things you can do for your child if she is in an online course is to print off the course calendar and help her break down tasks and manage due dates. Quizzes and tests are proctored online, or taken in person, or, at least, final exams or required state exams can be. This requirement depends on the organization from whom your child is taking the course. Sometimes a password is required for exams, and sometimes they are also timed. Organizations are required by law to make accommodations for students with most exceptional needs, but if your child is enrolled in a digital program outside of his or her school you need to make the program administrators aware of those needs when you register your child for the course. I will go more in depth on strategies for students with exceptional needs in Chapter 7.

In an ideal world, when a school has online classes, the school or online teacher should send home an email, a note, newsletter, or the school or teacher should host a parent meeting explaining to the parents the type of class and expectations that are in place. However, I have found that this isn't always the case. Unfortunately, what I normally see are schools that implement wonderful programs but forget the key component for success—parents.

This is one of my motivations in writing this book. Too many of us don't know how to help our children because schools aren't telling us how. They think because we know how to check our email or send text messages that we know how to help our kids with digital education. In actuality, digital education is very different than text messages or emails. Without the right knowledge it can be VERY frustrating. This frustration goes both ways. I have had conversations with many parents, where I pull up the statistics of an online course, and I say:

"Your daughter hasn't logged into her online class in four days. That is why she has a 52." Mom then says:

"Well, that isn't possible. She was on the computer all night."

Uhhmmm…There is a big difference in being on the computer and working in an online class. Just because your child is on the computer doesn't necessarily mean she is working in her class. The beauty of data is that it allows educators to capture individualized information. With many software packages, educators can see every click a child makes, which helps them diagnose learning weaknesses. This also tells them what time and, if or when, the child is working. This data also assists in identifying academic integrity issues—AKA—cheating.

Chapter 6 will help you with strategies for internet safety and balance. One such strategy is monitoring the screen of the device your child uses. It isn't the best idea to allow her to work from her bedroom (heard this already, huh?), where you cannot see her screen. It also isn't the best idea to have the wireless available past her bedtime. What is that you say? What about her phone, where she always has access? You can have her check it in at bed time or take advantage of the parental controls. Judgment weakens at night, and we find ourselves tempted to do things we wouldn't always do. This is compounded if your child is a teen. Remember the prefrontal cortex we discussed in chapter 2? Your teen's brain is fully developed to seek pleasure and rewards, but the area of his brain responsible for judgement isn't fully developed. A lapse in judgement only takes about three seconds when it comes to sending an inappropriate picture, but it will haunt a child for the remainder of her high school career in social media. See Chapter 5.

- **Flex Model** – In the flex model teachers use online classes as the primary form of instruction in order to provide individualized learning where students can work at their own pace. In this model, though, the teachers are accessible at the physical location of the school for face-to-face support. This support might include instruction for small groups, tutoring or opportunities for group projects. There is a lot of flexibility with this model based on how the school wants to design the structure.

- **A La Carte Model** – In this model you get a little sampling of everything! Students who are enrolled in a traditional school and may take one or two classes online while still taking other classes face-to-face are participating in an A La Carte model. Hypothetically, a student could be in a 1:1 environment, where the one teacher prefers station rotation while taking another class from a teacher who uses the flipped model. Meanwhile his 4th period teacher may just be doing really well to get the overhead lightbulb changed, and he might be able to come to school at 2nd period rather than 1st period to help with the school's overcrowding because he is taking one of his classes completely online.

- **<u>Enriched Virtual Model</u>** – Remember the young man who I just described that was taking an online class from home because the school was overcrowded? This helped him anyway because he really isn't a morning person. Let's say the teacher for the online course also works at the school, and he has to check in with her once a week. In this situation, his online class is considered "enriched" because he isn't working on it 100% online without seeing his teacher. It isn't a flipped classroom because he isn't meeting with his teacher everyday either.

In Appendix G, I provide some key questions you may want to ask your child's teacher when beginning the transition to a digital classroom.

STUDENT STORY

When David entered 6th grade he was behind in math. He was so far behind that he tested on the 2nd grade-level based on the California state assessments, but he wanted to be an engineer. His 6th grade teacher used a software program, Prodigy, that is free to educators (fee for parents). Students take a diagnostic test at the beginning so that the software will know exactly where their strengths and weaknesses are. Then the software adapts and creates an individualized pathway for each student. The math problems are gamified, and using a wizard theme, which is perfect for middle school, students are immersed in edutainment. David, who LOVED video games, raised his math state testing from 2nd grade level to 8thgrade level, which is unheard of. His teacher was thrilled with his success, and this drastic change in his skillset completely changed the trajectory of his behavioral and academic career.

CHAPTER 4
MY CHILD'S TEACHER, AN ENVIRONMENTALIST: DOES HE REALLY NOT HAVE A TEXTBOOK?

All children are different. When my sister and I would come home from school if you asked my sister what she did you'd get a, "Nothin'," but if you asked me you'd get the day in a word-by-word recap. If you happen to have a child like my sister, no matter how you ask the question you won't get the details of the day, and eventually you feel disconnected. Traditionally, you could have resorted to folders and textbooks to try and gather details from the curriculum to determine what your child was doing in school, but in a digital classroom, there may not be a textbook or paper folders to root through.

DOES YOUR CHILD NEED A
TEXTBOOK TO LEARN?

So, does this digital transition in education just mean more of a disconnected society? Absolutely not! It is actually the opposite! Instead, you may actually be able to log into a digital class and see everything that took place that day. You may be able to see the vocabulary words yourself even if your child lost them or supposedly "doesn't have any this week." Oh, and what if your son forgot his textbook, but he is supposed to read tonight and answer chapter questions? That clever trick may not work anymore like it did when you were in school! With digital resources, while it feels very different than what you may have experienced, it is actually easier to connect with the teacher and see what is due; when things are due; what resources are being used; how your child is performing; and where to access activities.

But…how do children learn if they don't have traditional textbooks? On the one hand, a huge problem is solved. Remember all of the hoopla in the media a few years back about how heavy textbooks were? Well, it was real. Students were being asked to carry up to twenty pounds in their backpacks by the time they had all of their books and band instruments loaded on their backs. This is simply too much, and it can cause chronic pain and complications. Obviously, technology provides a solution to this, but just like we invested in backpacks with wheels for our children when we had concerns about the weight they were lugging around on their backs, we also have to be proactive with technology. For example, some of you may be worried about devices being stolen, cyber bullying, stalkers etc., and this is why it is crucial for parents to be even more involved and to be proactive when it comes to technology in the classroom. So, save their backs while watching their backs, which is why we will discuss Online Safety in Chapter 5.

Let's talk about your school experience. In most cases there was probably a textbook involved. Textbooks are a very profitable business. Traditionally, a team of teachers, the textbook committee, reviews the textbook materials, over a nice lunch provided by the textbook vendor and votes on one company from which to adopt the textbooks. Don't get me wrong, not all teachers only teach straight from the textbook, but most of your teachers probably did.

Now, let's talk about how you learn. These are fun facts to know:

- People remember 90% of what they say and do.

- We remember 30% of what we see and hear (Asselin & Mooney, 1996).

Hmmmmm…Now you know why all those lectures were so boring. Should your child be reading a textbook and listening to a lecture, or should your child be participating in something like I previously described with the Pythagorean theorem? Maybe this digital learning environment, where your child can manipulate objects without fear of failure, isn't such a bad idea. Why is it more engaging to manipulate objects via technology rather than the real thing?

As a learning strategy, integrating technology can effectively promote learning. Studies have shown significant success in 1:1 programs, which is where each child has a device to use in class (Horn & Staker 2014). When programs are implemented with specific educational guidance, teachers see fewer discipline problems and dropout rates decrease. Furthermore, more students go to college who participate in 1:1 environments than in other blended programs, where students may work in groups, sharing computers, or where they may not be in a 1:1 environment. It is important to note that in digital settings, even without 1:1 device ratios, one study found 69% of schools reported their students' scores on high-stakes tests increased (Roblyer & Doering, 2013). The keys to successful blended learning are to know all the ins and outs and to be able to support both your child and the teacher since they interact differently than in the traditional classroom.

A great example of a digital learning environment can be seen at Mooresville High School in North Carolina. Through a six-year process, they eliminated the use of static textbooks. They now use all digital activities with their students. This process has led their students to increase overall test scores an average of 25 points from 64% to 89%! Students are engaged, and teachers are well-trained in how to integrate the technology. Discipline problems have decreased, and the technology integration has led Mooresville to the highest graduate rates for African American students in the state of North Carolina (Florence & Hamilton, 2014). The point is, there is something to this digital stuff. It is good for kids.

Reach around and pat yourself on the back. Parenting isn't easy, and you are making the choices that will, according to scientific research, make the difference in your child's digital educational experience by reading this book. The next step will be to apply what you learn. Hmmm… seems like you are also a student.

Whether your child's teacher or school is at the beginning, middle, or top of the spectrum for implementing digital curriculum, you and your child will benefit if implementation includes all stakeholders, and the teachers are well-prepared. This is mainly because children are engaged and learning can be personalized to their individualized needs.

Although I'm not suggesting traditional textbooks be replaced with PDF documents or electronic textbooks, it is imperative that we dissect what happens when we interact with electronic text. As parents, it is important to understand how you can help your child improve in these skills.

DIGITAL LITERACY

Whether in experiential learning or active learning, when your children go to websites or are manipulating software to actively learn, their brains are engaging differently than when they read paper-based materials. Specifically, when you read online you train your brain to read differently; therefore, you interact differently with text. Instead of reading from left to right and searching for details in text, you skim and jump from topic to topic on the page. That's right, reading online trains our brains to read differently (Carr, 2011). When you don't find what you are looking for, you go to the next site—immediate gratification. Remember the characteristics of Gen Z, and remember that teen brain? It is almost as if you are searching for answers or rewards instead of thinking. You may hear educators refer to this kind of literacy as technical literacy (or technical literacy skill), which is just as important to our youth when preparing a 21st century global workforce as the traditional literacy skills we had to learn.

With traditional literacy, you read from left to right and top to bottom; there is a process, and you digest or comprehend as you read through one-way communication. Sure, you scan the paper-based text, but not like you do online. When you read on paper, you don't close the window when you can't find the answer or hop to a new resource within fifteen seconds. With digital literacy all of the resources you are reading are also networked, and nothing is static. The experience is totally different.

Most often you look at widgets on a screen for key words that have been identified by search engines to save you time. Content is presented in a fragmented way since you may see video, images, text, audio, advertisements and or an RSS feed (when updates automatically happen on the page), to name a few. These are all presented in various forms on one screen. You can imagine the different skills needed to process the information presented in this way instead of concentrating on a process of flow of language on a piece of paper. There is a lot of information to digest at one time, and we do it at a rapid pace since search engines make the availability of information much easier and quicker.

Your child needs to utilize both technical and traditional literacy skills in order to be successful in both a digital classroom and in a global workforce. This may be difficult since children in our country suffer poor literacy skills. Unfortunately, about 20 percent of Americans age 15 and older lack basic functional literacy skills and are twice as likely to drop out of school, according to an assessment by the United Nations (Kanj & Mitic, 2009). I have included suggestions for helping your children navigate and better comprehend in both the digital and traditional environments in Appendix F.

The good news is, while children learn to comprehend in different ways, they are motivated to learn these technical literacy skills. This is because technology, when implemented correctly, can be a motivator. The key to all of this, of course, is the teacher. She is a digital immigrant, as opposed to your child, who is a digital native. Despite this, she must be well-trained and know how to implement the technology correctly to motivate and engage your child. In a digital classroom, there is a balance of student motivation, good instruction, teacher efficacy, classroom management, climate, and many more variables that I won't bore you with any more educator speak.

In a digital environment, teachers have more curriculum options than in a traditional classroom. They can select different websites, different resources, or various materials because they have a wider variety from which to choose materials to meet your child's needs. In the digital environment each teacher gets to select every individual material she uses. What does this mean? Well, it means that teachers need to be experts in curriculum resources, and they need more time than ever before, which isn't going to happen, because we know teachers continue to have more mandates added to their task list daily. Conversely, it means they need to work together to share resources. Why re-invent the wheel? When one teacher finds a great resource, she needs to share it with another. It is possible that a teacher may not be using the best site in existence, and you need to be aware of that when you help your child with homework or a class activity. Remember your child's teacher may be writing curriculum as well as managing a full load of students.

If you find useful sites to aid with class assignments, you may want to reach out to your PTA and start a community page or blog. Just like teachers, parents are also searching for helpful resources. There is no sense in 20 parents searching for a good site on multiplying fractions on the same night. Again, why reinvent the wheel? Share. All of us want the same thing, for our children to be successful. If you and your child find a great site to help translate Shakespeare, and you find out what, "Wherefore art thou Romeo?" really means, by all means share because we all know Juliet isn't really asking where he is, as most students think.

Starting a community like this also helps answer questions like, how do I know if the website I'm looking at is a good site or if it is teaching the way my child's teacher teaches? I have included suggestions for selecting credible websites in Appendix E. I also keep an updated list of recommended resources on my website: www.DrWendyOliver.com.

What is that you say? Oh, I have made an assumption. Some of you reading this book are overachievers, and you are preparing for when your child is in a digital classroom. Others of you are desperately seeking help, because you are in the middle of a meltdown. For those of you who haven't experienced the dreaded 6th grade math worksheet with no examples and no textbook to look at for examples; you may not know why you'd be looking frantically for a website at 9:30 pm on Thursday night after a basketball game or 10 pm Sunday night when your child confesses, after coming home from her father's, that she didn't do her homework yet.

You get the picture. Your 6th grader is new to this type of learning. She is also new to learning to middle school, which means learning to be responsible. Meanwhile, you have to relearn 6th grade math, which is very different than it was when you were in 6th grade (we won't discuss how long ago that was). So, how do you jolt your brain to help her, without yelling and losing your patience or writing an ugly note to the teacher for not sending home examples (because I know that is what you will want to do)?

SOME TIPS FOR THE WORKSHEET

- Be proactive. Go to the teacher's website if he or she has one and search around for any clues.

- Unless the teacher created the worksheet herself, it is likely that the name of the website where the worksheet was created is marked on the page somewhere.

- Go to a search engine and look up the key words from the worksheet. Ask your child what she is studying. Are you looking at order of operations?

If it is English, are you working on subject/verb agreement? Usually the directions are a give-away.

- Type one of the questions into a search engine.

- NEVER pay for a website to help you.

- Is there a log in you need to access the curriculum for parents? You may need to ask the teacher this at the beginning of the year or when you realize worksheets are being sent home with no other support.

- Write the teacher a note. Be NICE! Ask her if she provided additional resources to your child should he or she have difficulties. Tell her all of the sites you tried, and that you could not find a good resource to help you. Ask the teacher to provide you with resources that will help so you can tutor your child. Also, ask for extra time since you did not find these resources, even with diligent effort.

If the problem persists, ask the teacher if she would consider providing some links to resources she finds credible, or where you can look for assistance on assignments when helping your child. Perhaps you can help him by recommending, creating, or modifying an existing "parents" section to his website to improve the blended or online portion of the class.

YOU HAVE TALKED A LOT ABOUT MATH, BUT WHAT ABOUT SCIENCE?

I'm sure you have no problem with your child not inhaling formaldehyde, but is a simulated frog dissection, one you do online, just as good as dissecting a real frog? My response to that is: it is six of one and a half-dozen of the other. In 2009 The College Board ruled that simulated labs were not as effective as real-world labs, so students participating in AP courses needed to participate in hands-on experiments rather than simulated ones in order to get college credit.

Schools, though, are very interested in using simulated labs. When I ran The State of Tennessee's online program, I couldn't figure out why the students in a district in West Tennessee were skipping all of the labs in the science classes. After further investigation, I found out that although the state required lab work for all of the classes, because the district didn't have funding for labs, students in the district weren't used to doing them. As a result, they weren't completing the labs in the online class.

Across the nation, schools have cut labs from their budgets, even in life sciences, because, believe it or not, dead worms and frogs cost money. So, you tell me, parents…Would you prefer your child not have the experience of dissecting, in a society where they need STEM (Science, Technology Math, Engineering and Math) skills to be successful? Or would you prefer they miss out on the formaldehyde experience in order to have the opportunity to practice the experience digitally?

In a simulated environment, the required space or equipment to dissect the creatures isn't necessary. Also, the danger factor is removed. You don't have to worry about your child cutting his thumb when slicing open a fish. In either method, hands-on or simulated, The Scientific Method can and should be employed by your child, which is critical for the learning experience. Dissecting a real frog is no better than clicking through an online dissection if your child is not required to think and draw conclusions during the process. To be prepared to compete in a 21st century global economy students do need the experience of simulated labs, and there are a variety of ways to do this while even including real-world labs.

I have included great sites with science and math simulations you may want to explore in the Appendix D. Remember, we learn best by *doing*.

HOW TO SELECT A GOOD WEBSITE

So, you found a phenomenal resource that gives you the exact information you need online. You must remember that basically anyone can publish on the internet, except maybe your neighbor's dog. You also need to remember you aren't exactly searching the library when you are on Google. So, use the following guide to see if that site your son wants to use for his English homework passes the test for being credible. Also, remember that Wikipedia is not considered to be a credible academic citation. It is open source, which means anyone can contribute. This means that even if you aren't an expert on a subject you can post information for the world to consume.

- What is the date on the website or article? Has it been updated recently? Are the links up to date and working?

- Who is the author of the information you are reading? Is it someone credible? Superman isn't really a credible source on kryptonite since he is fictitious, for example. Or is he? If you saw Kris Kringle listed as the author of a page on the origin of Easter, you could gather that the source isn't very credible.

- Are there citations for any references the author uses?

- Are there any clues that the author is biased? For example, is the author promoting a product? If so, then move along to the next site. Ideally the author will appear unbiased and credible.

- Does the site look like something you'd find in the library rather than an advertisement?

In addition to the above discovery list, the following information about domain names may be helpful when determining the credibility of a website.

- .edu = education sites

- .gov = government sites

- .org= organization sites

- .com = commercial sites

- .net = network infrastructures

In combination with the discoveries you made when going through the checklist above, review the domain name. For example, if your site is an education site or government site, it will likely provide credible information. At times, grant funded sites may be out of date, so it is still important to go through the checklist provided. I suggest you try to find resources on sites that end in .edu, .gov, and/or .org for academic work. Even the sites I recommend may be broken in the near future, which is why I keep an updated list on my website.

SUGGESTED SITES FOR INTERACTIVE CONTENT ACTIVITIES

Millions of parents, teachers and students visit these open source sites a month to get ideas and assistance with homework, lesson plans and projects. Please remember, that your data may be tracked in exchanged for "free" resources. If you click on "I agree" in exchange for usage, you may be agreeing to allow the organization to sell your data to a 3rd party (it pays to read the fine print), and not all sites are created equal.

STUDENT STORY

Ryan was a brilliant young man. As a matter of fact, he graduated from high school at twelve years old. The school district struggled to find resources to challenge him. The only solution was to allow him to take advanced classes online that the school didn't offer and to advance and graduate early. Once he was in high school, though, he was required to take physical education in order to graduate. The school and Ryan's mother were concerned that older students would pick on him in physical education, and Ryan, understandably, didn't want to change clothes in front of high school students. In order to protect his safety and allow him to graduate early with a diploma, Ryan took PE online. He loved it, and the solution was ideal for all involved.

CHAPTER 5
HOW DO I COMMUNICATE WITH A "DIGITAL TEACHER"?

Hmmm…What does an open house or a parent-teacher conference look like if your child's teacher is online? If the school has gone 1:1 (where every child uses a device—see Chapter 3). Does the school still have an open house? These are legitimate questions as you engage in the digital learning model. Fortunately, schools that incorporate digital strategies aren't quite up to the standard of the Jetsons, but they are definitely moving away from the Flintstone age!

Like we discussed in Chapter 3, today's classroom is quite different than the classroom we, as parents, learned in. Remember this is a good thing, but school is still about one thing—students. As a parent, it is your job to be your child's biggest advocate. That stated, how do you communicate with your child's teacher in this changing landscape? How do you communicate with a teacher you cannot see at drop-off or pick-up? If your child is learning in a 100% online course, will you meet/talk with the online teacher? If so, how?

ONLINE PLATFORM

Actually, it is much easier than you think. Many teachers who use digital tools with their instruction are very efficient with their communication. Believe it or not, their feedback can also be really personalized. The first thing to do is determine if your child's digital class is taking place in an online portal. An online portal is where the content is delivered. In other words, does your child log in to a secure system that tracks all of his work for the class? If so, your child will be given a specific set of login credentials that is unique to him when the teacher begins using the online program. Ideally, at the beginning of the year or when the teacher begins using digital tools, the school or teacher should send you information for a parent account that will also give you access to the system. This information should provide:

- Secure login address
- User ID
- Password

Let's imagine you logged in without any glitches the first time. Go you! Now what?

Even though all learning platforms are different, each typically has the same core functionality. Think of a recipe. A cake usually has sugar, butter, eggs, and flour. Even though a rum cake has something different in it to give it an extra zing, most all cakes have the same core ingredients. Good learning platforms typically have tabs or buttons that represent: Communication, Gradebook, Curriculum, and Course Information.

Now that you are logged in, you need to determine how the teacher prefers to give and receive communication from parents and students. In the best scenario, you and your child will receive a welcome email or a phone call from the teacher that tells you this, but if you don't it should also be posted in the course. If the course has just started, then you may see this information in an announcement, or if the course has been in session for a bit, then I'd suggest reviewing the course syllabus for the teacher's contact information. Usually the syllabus can be found in Course Information or something with a similar title. Here you can find answers to some of the following questions:

- Is the teacher accessible for re-teaching or is tutoring offered?

- What are the contact hours and numbers or email to use?

- Can my child work ahead?

- How will I know if my child gets behind?

- What are the consequences for getting behind?

- Is there an orientation? If not/if so, how will I know where the resources are?

- Does my child have a balance of screen time with off-screen assignments?

- Does my child have to do something different for proctored tests to log in?

If you don't see answers to these questions upon login, they are great questions to ask the teacher as soon as possible.

Logging in will either be a breeze, or it will be a nightmare. If all else fails, ask your child for assistance. There is no shame in this. Actually, if you have difficulty logging in, make sure your CapsLock isn't on. If you still cannot login, there should be a button to select for password help or a button to select for technical support. If you don't see those options, then it is a good thing you purchased this book and are reading Chapter 5 because you will need to communicate with the teacher. I just did this for my daughter's online math homework program this year, when my first two passwords issued by the school would not provide me access to the course.

In this situation, because I could not access the online homework portal, I spoke to my daughter's teacher in person when I dropped her off. Since my daughter is in elementary school, and the digital math program is used in a blended model classroom, it was very easy to communicate with her teacher face-to-face. Other options I had were to call the school and discuss my technical problems, or I could have entered a help desk ticket in the online portal to ask for assistance with my log in. I could have also emailed the teacher, text her, or called her, as I have all of these forms of communication from her as options for preferred methods of communication.

Fortunately, my daughter's teacher prefers to over-communicate. She also uses an app called ClassTag, which is a free app (supported by advertisers), where she sends announcements and pictures of the students working and playing to the parents in the class. Other teachers may have another preferred method of communication. They will make this clear to students, as well as, their times of availability.

COMMUNICATING WITH THE TEACHER IN AN ONLINE CLASS

It may seem odd, but it isn't uncommon for teachers to prefer text messages. Teachers lead busy lives, and they have their own families to tend to after hours. They still want to be available to support their students, though. Don't be alarmed if your child tells you that his or her teacher allows texting for questions with homework assignments after school. Texting is a quick method of communication for teachers and students. Texting is informal and may create a relationship to develop that is more congenial with students and teachers over time. A strong rapport with students and teachers is extremely important, but your judgement as a parent is essential regarding appropriateness and etiquette. I highly suggest you monitor texts with teachers with the same diligence you do with friends and other adults. Children should be respectful and have boundaries as far as appropriate times to text teachers, and they should maintain a level of respect appropriate for the classroom, just as teachers should maintain an appropriate level of professionalism.

Not all teachers prefer text messaging. In an online class, a teacher may say that she is available for "office hours" during specific times and certain days. During this time, she may be available for live chat or phone calls. Another way to say this is that the teacher is directly accessible to work with students during this window of time. If the teacher prefers a phone call, then during the hours and days posted, she is available by phone for a conversation. If the teacher prefers live chat, then instructions for live chat, such as Skype, Zoom, or a similar service may be scheduled. If provided by the course platform, you might see invitations from Adobe Connect or WebeX. During these sessions, students log in with their devices, mobile, or computer, and talk face-to-face over the internet with their teachers. There is usually a function where each person can share his or her screen to demonstrate work or show examples. Sometimes there is a "whiteboard" function, where teachers can show their screens to students and "write/type" on the screen. This is ideal for math sessions, for example. Teachers may even have traditional whiteboards on their videos. During live lessons, teachers usually use this function to join multiple students in order to allow for collaboration.

Live, or synchronous, lessons allow students to interact and collaborate with one another, as well as, experience social interaction and diversity in an online course. Student-to-student interaction and student-to-teacher interaction are both critical to a student's learning. Think back to group projects you may have done in school or when the teacher may have led a group discussion. These types of assignments are similar to the experiences you had in the traditional classroom. If your child is taking online classes only and not participating in any traditional classes, then you will want to make sure the curriculum has multiple opportunities for collaboration with other students, the community, and the teacher.

Although we heard the stories of how our grandparents walked a mile or more in the snow one way to school, we did actually play outside. At least some of us did, depending on age. In the digital age, children grow up in a media-rich environment and are essentially immersed in digital worlds from birth. This means that digital media may replace the traditional activity, such as playing outside or hands-on learning, both of which are critical to development.

When teachers expand their instruction to include digital opportunities, they expand their classroom to include the world. For example, I have worked with some schools (even elementary), that connect with other classrooms internationally via Skype. This allows children to communicate with other students across the globe without geographical barriers. Digital collaboration provides the opportunity for your child to learn more about the world rather than just their local community.

Expanding assignments to include the local community is another great way for students to be inspired in a digital environment. If they complete the work offline, they can make connections to the local community while balancing their screen time. An experienced teacher or a strong curriculum will be able to achieve this balance. As a parent, you can help make this connection for your child by connecting the work she is doing in the digital environment to your local community or the national or even international community. This makes for great conversation during dinner since it might be a "No Phone Zone." Trust me, your teenagers will appreciate this boundary…eventually. Believe it or not, they are begging for boundaries.

Perhaps you are reading this book because you received an email or voicemail something like this:

Ms. Ryans,

I would like to schedule a 20-minute meeting with you during parent conferences next week. Zach hasn't been turning in his math homework, and I'm concerned regarding his failing grade. You should have access to his grades in the online gradebook of his class if you have any questions.

Sincerely,

Teacher

Let's fast forward to the conference.

Teacher: Ms. Ryans, I'm so glad you could make it. Zach's attendance is good, but he never has his homework. Homework is 40% of his grade.

Ms. Ryans: I'm really confused, he is always on the computer at night doing his homework. Last night he was on the computer for at least two hours. He told me he was doing math homework.

Teacher: Really? Let me log in and see how much time he spent in his class last night doing the homework. Pause. See this chart, Ms. Ryans? This shows me when he logged in last and for how long he was logged in. It also tells me where he clicked in the course. It is somewhat like big brother, but from this I can tell that he didn't log in last night.

Ms. Ryans (Shocked!): He is dead meat!

If you re-read what Ms. Ryans said, you will notice that her son, Zach, was on the computer. She didn't say she saw him doing his math homework. It sounds like Ms. Ryans has a pretty smart son, who is a typical teenager. I don't blame him. I'd rather chat with my friends or play an online game than do math homework too.

In chapter 5, I talk about internet safety and having the screen that your child is using visible to an adult. This is another reason why a screen or monitor a child or teenager is using should always be visible to an adult. Ms. Ryans didn't necessarily need to sit down beside Zach. He could have been doing his math at the kitchen table while she made dinner. This would have allowed her to get her tasks done, and it would have required him to stay focused on his math.

Did you also wonder if Ms. Ryans knew she had access to her son's grades in the online gradebook prior to the email? In this example, she may not have even known she could look online to view her son's grades. Or, maybe the teacher sent something home that never actually made it. Another scenario is that she may have "heard" something about checking grades online, but she may not have known how to actually do so.

In the above example I changed the names "to protect the innocent." I have actually had many conversations around the potential scenarios I suggested as options for Ms. Ryans with parents as they embark on the journey of digital education. As an administrator, I have also had the difficult conversation I described between Ms. Ryans and the teacher many times with parents who thought their child was doing homework because the child said he or she was online. It is important to remember that a digital footprint is forever. What does this mean? Everything students do digitally leaves data. When used appropriately, to ask the parent to intervene and monitor a child in order to improve his academic success, data is extremely helpful.

ONLINE GRADEBOOK

Another way data can be very helpful in the digital environment is for grading. Because many digital assignments are automatically graded by the computer, you and your child can immediately be updated and know academic progress just by logging in to the gradebook. Remember running to the bulletin board or by the classroom door to see what your score was on a test? Or remember waiting days or even weeks for an assignment to be graded? With digital assignments, most quizzes and tests are graded by the computer and automatically posted to the gradebook. This makes life easier for everyone. There are, of course, exceptions to this. There is software available that is still being tested to grade essays. While it can assess grammar, artificial intelligence software isn't quite fancy enough to see if a student wrote what the teacher intended. The same goes for grading projects or anything creative, authentic or real-world. These types of assignments still require the teacher's time and expertise. Teachers will always be needed and should never be replaced.

So, what should you do if you have a question about a grade you see in the online gradebook? You should talk to, call, text, or email the teacher.

A sample email could look something like this:

Dear Ms. Teacher,

I was reviewing Zach's gradebook last night, and I'm concerned that he has three low grades in a row. It looks, from the calendar, that the unit test is coming up. Will you be offering any tutoring sessions? What do you suggest? He and I don't think he is ready for the test.

Appreciatively,

Madison Ryans
615-444-1223

ADAPTIVE TECHNOLOGIES

This is where things begin to get interesting. There are some programs that introduce machine learning into digital classes. In these systems, predictive algorithms can detect that, in this case, Zach has missed a skill five times. This means he needs some additional practice on this specific skill. As a result, the system will "feed" him extra practice on this skill. Another example might be that the system detects patterns in Zach's answers similar to other students who performed a certain way on the test, so it "feeds" him extra practice on things they missed because his data looks like theirs. Think of this like Netflix or your recommendations on Amazon. You have recommended shows to watch based on what you have watched in the past or recommended purchases based on your previous purchases.

Is this meant to replace the teacher? Absolutely not. This is meant to give your child extra support "just in time," as he needs it. This technology provides a personalized learning pathway specifically for your child. Within this type of technology, no two children have the exact same curriculum because their needs are different. Of course, a teacher is still needed. Who would answer questions?

Well…in some digital curriculum, artificial intelligence (AI) tutors, like when you saw IBM's Watson win at Jeopardy, are actually answering questions. A bank of questions and responses are built, and the AI gets smarter and smarter over time, continually building the bank of knowledge for the computer. The purpose of these technologies should not be to replace a teacher. Rather, they should be to reduce lower-level tasks and free the teacher up, so that she can spend more time one-on-one with your child. As your child's advocate, you should expect deeper engagement with teachers and deeper learning if digital curriculum offers all of these advanced technologies. Also, pay particular attention to data and privacy policies.

STUDENT STORY

Chloe was a competitive gymnast who practiced four hours a day. Her schedule was intense. Plus, she traveled to competitions, which caused her to miss school. She enrolled in online classes, which allowed her to take school with her. She could complete her schoolwork and study at times that worked within her schedule. Chloe competed in the junior Olympics and maintained a 4.0 GPA.

CHAPTER 6
ONLINE SAFETY: IS IT REALLY SAFE?

When I first started Tennessee's online learning program I had to be careful not to use the term *virtual*. Instead, I had to be conscientious and use the term *online learning*. You are probably reading this and wondering what the difference is. In 2005, many people associated the term virtual with games and inappropriate online behavior. The terms were not synonymous, nor was virtual common to education. Parents associated bad things happening to their children in virtual environments.

They were right. Bad things can happen to children in virtual environments, but bad things can happen to children in online environments too because they are the same thing. I know that you have been online and seen inappropriate images or language, be they intentional or not. I remember when I was teaching 9th grade English I researched the book *Animal Farm*, by typing the title into a search engine. I will not go into detail, but I can tell you I was mortified by the images that came up. I was doing a legitimate search, and the inappropriate images are forever imprinted on my brain. I had been married for less than a month, and I was twenty-three years old. If I, an adult who is now an expert in online learning, made that mistake, then what will our children do as they learn to navigate their way around the internet?

We all know technology isn't going away. Simply put, the convenience and the resources provided by the internet offer more educational benefits than consequences. We have to educate ourselves and our children of the best ways to avoid incidents such as my *Animal Farm* experience. Trust me. You don't want to see what I saw. I know you have to wonder how you will completely immerse your child into the digital world, while you balance safety and the real-world. After all, as parents we have to worry enough about providing a safe environment in the real world for our children. Now we are tossing the digital world into the realm of worry too. You don't need medication to calm you down, and you don't need more hours in a day, I promise. As it is with everything, though, knowledge is power. One of the challenges about children being in digital learning environments is that you, as a parent, need to make sure you are ready to take on the level of engagement that is required to keep them safe. If we make modifications and digital learning a team effort, not only will the education experience improve, but we will also equip our children with a stronger foundation in digital literacy. As discussed previously, digital literacy will, most certainly, impact their adult lives for the better.

Before you can go to bat for internet safety, though, you need to know who your opponent is. You also need to remember children are online for reasons other than school. They probably have been online a fair amount before you began reading this book. Buckle your seatbelt because even as I write this my parental protective radar is in high gear. Let's begin with some statistics.

ONLINE PREDATORS

There are 900,000 children "criminally mistreated each year, and as of 2018 there were 747, 408 registered sex offenders in the United States (Dillinger, 2018). According to the FBI there are approximately 50,000 predators online at any given moment, looking for victims (Child Rescue Network, 2019). Yet schools encourage us to have our children online for homework and schoolwork rather than using or in addition to a textbook. What gives? Remember, in Chapter 2 when I told you that Gen Z spends 8-9 hours connected? Trust me. That isn't all for schoolwork. This is a topic you are probably already be dealing with, but until now you may not have been aware how risky being online really is.

Many teenagers play games online, where these 50,000 predators can easily access their personal information, especially since 27% of teens play games online with people they don't know (Netzsmartz, 2019). Think about this: whether your child is playing on an Xbox or a Playstation, or even a Wii, the gaming devices connect through a television and WiFi. They also have cameras, which are used in order to actually play the game and to communicate with other people when the compete online in groups. What this means is that your child, while playing his game, is an easy target. Predators are smart; they will pretend to be younger than they are, acting as though they are kids. If I haven't scared you enough keep reading... (2) Approximately one in five teenagers has received an unsolicited sexual exploitation online, and only one of those five has told an adult (Pure Sight, 2019). Do the math on that. Now, if I hadn't convinced you to move the devices out of their bedrooms yet, I have no doubt those two statistics did! And if they didn't, this will: One in 25 teenagers received a sexual solicitation online, where the predator tried to meet them in person somewhere. Think about that for a few minutes. That is at least one child from every classroom in America!

Let me also clarify that online means a lot more than on the computer. Remember that when your children are on their smartphones, they are usually online, and the 50,000-predator statistic applies there too. So, let's talk about smartphones, which are really mini-computers with GPS devices. When we were in school, we had to be conscientious of ruining our reputations with rumors based on our activities, where people from school would see us. Remember, it was okay to go hang out with your parents on a Friday night, as long as nobody from school saw you. Now, though, there is the issue with digital footprints, as I mentioned earlier, or digital data, that creates permanent pictures and documentation trails associated with text messages and social media.

SOCIAL MEDIA

No matter how an app is described, digital data never goes away. It is critical that you have conversations with your child about the responsibility that comes with having a digital device, boundaries, and her own digital footprint. I specifically chose the feminine pronoun "her" regarding a digital footprint because although 95% of kids have smartphones, as of 2018 and 45% of them say they are on them constantly. Girls are more likely to use social media than boys. The three most popular social media sites in the US currently are YouTube, Instagram, and Snapchat (Anderson & Jiang, 2018). All of these sites use images for content. Images that are user created with the cameras on smartphones. Remember that the digital footprint never goes away, and nothing digital is ever private, even if your child thinks it "disappears" after seconds or after she "takes it down."

Why did I mention that the images are coming from their smartphones? All digital images are geotagged. This means that the latitude and longitude of where the photo is taken is stored in the metadata of the image. Sometimes social media sites remove this data in order to make the file smaller when you upload it but not always. Either way, it is simple to recover the data. If you have your family's picture set as your Facebook profile, and your child is in a school uniform, how hard would it be for a predator to find your child knowing this information, especially since your Facebook photo cannot be anonymous unless you block a specific individual?

Step 1. Talk to your child about her digital footprint.

Step 2. Change your profile picture on Facebook.

Step 3. Go into the app for your and your child's cameras and turn off the location settings.

There are countless examples of girls who send "nudes" to what they think is a trusting boyfriend. If they are sending this to an actual "friend" they know from school, then at least you know the other human involved. If they are sending the "nude" to a "friend" or "follower" online, then you should be very suspicious, for depending on the social media site, remember, an adult can be impersonating a teenager.

If you aren't familiar, a "nude" is an image of a private area of the body that someone sends to another. This is almost an epidemic in middle and high schools, and it is leading to a lot of harassment, anxiety, and embarrassment in teens. Even worse, the bullying that has developed as a result has led to suicides across the country (Sales, 2016). A girl will volunteer or be pressured into sending a nude image to a boy, thinking it will gain his favor, and he will then send the picture(s) to multiple friends. Before long, the entire school has seen the picture(s), and the original sender becomes the center of attention for all the wrong reasons. Other examples include, teenagers putting nude pictures on social media simply to get extra "likes" or "hits" because this is a measure of popularity. If your child is on Instagram, anyone can see what she posts and find her location, and Snapchat never really goes away.

If their digital footprint isn't enough of a concern, let's talk about the permanency of a criminal record. What if your daughter, who is under 18 willingly sends a picture of her breasts to her boyfriend? She could be charged with production of child pornography, felony possession of child pornography, and felony trafficking of child pornography" (Weinberger, 2017, p. 123). You guessed it. If her boyfriend keeps the picture or shares it with others, he too can be charged with felony possession and trafficking of child pornography. Two middle schoolers in Indiana, one 12 and the other 13, were charged with possession of child pornography and child exploitation for exchanging nude images of themselves. Their lives will never be the same.

Step 4. Discuss the implications of sexting and sending nudes.

Why on Earth would kids do this sort of thing? You know you raised them better, right? Our culture has desensitized sexuality. The very thought of teen girls sending nudes for popularity makes the feminist in me want to scream. It's as if we are going backwards in time, yet girls are doing this to themselves. Remember that the worst combination of developed v. underdeveloped parts of their brain spells T-R-O-U-B-L-E when it comes to independence and online identity. Teens are seeking pleasure, and they have no impulse control. Whether they like it or not, they need you to be engaged in their digital footprint (personal and academic) to help them make mature decisions.

Step 5. Monitor their phones regularly.

Step 6. Engage in their social media.

If a kid sends one sketchy picture, it can be forwarded around the entire school within minutes and even posted on social media sites. In other words, one lapse in judgment can become a permanent scar, especially since 15% of teens say they have received nude or semi-nude pictures of friends via text (Netsmartz, 2019).

In case you aren't familiar with Snapchat, let's revisit it. Snapchat is an app that deletes the picture as soon as the person receiving the picture opens it. On the one hand, this solves the problem of ruining your reputation as the evidence is immediately deleted (unless you are with law enforcement, who can recover it); however, it increases the anonymity, which encourages risqué behavior. It also decreases the opportunity for parental monitoring. In other words, your child might feel safer sending a nude picture since the receiver cannot forward it, and you will definitely never know that she did. Now, what if that nude picture was sent to a predator who was impersonating a kid your child's age? Because, guess what? Over half of kids sexually solicited online were asked to send a picture (Enough Is Enough, 2019).

CYBERBULLYING

Let's not overlook cyberbullying. Kids can be very cruel. You thought you made it through the bullying years of elementary school? Oh no...this is a whole new realm. Cyberbullying is bullying that takes place using a digital device. In 2007, Lenhart found that one in three teens had been cyberbullied. In 2019, 87% of young people have seen cyberbullying online (Broadbandsearch.com). It almost sounds silly to us since we experienced REAL bullying with REAL people on the playground or in the halls, but to this generation online bullying is just as real. Remember the saying sticks and stones? Well, it isn't true. Sixty-four percent of students say they do not feel safe at school because of cyberbullying, and most of it takes place over social media. Someone can make threats, mean comments, and/or intentionally exclude or threaten someone. Think about it. How much easier is it to be mean to someone if you don't have to face them?

Speaking of, have you heard of Ask.fm? This is a social media site where people anonymously ask other users questions or make anonymous comments. I'm not sure who thought this would be a good idea, but your child has no business on this site. It is a recipe for disaster for a child or teenager who is impressionable or looking for validation. Remember, kids can be mean, especially when they are hiding behind a computer. Anything where the interaction is anonymous is never a good idea. Your child may or may not be interacting with a child, first of all, and very hurtful things can be said. Ask.fm also allows for images to be posted, which is very concerning, given the ability for anonymous viewing and interaction. Ask. fm has been highly criticized as the platform that has been responsible for the communications that have led to several teen suicides. This is not a site I'd recommend you allow your child. There is certainly no educational benefit.

Opportunities for inappropriate behavior are all around your children given that any form of electronic communication allows for it. Remember that they can get online with their gaming systems too, which may be through the television, not just their computers. I can go on and on, but your parental paranoia is now officially on high alert, as you begin to think of all the ways your child or children communicate(s) digitally. This stuff is really scary. So, what do we do as parents to not only protect, but also teach them how to interact, when playing, socializing, or learning in digital environments? Minding your manners has taken on a whole new meaning for Gen Z and going digital is truly a joint effort between parents and the school. Here are some ways we can take back some of the risk.

CREATE AN OPEN LOCATION FOR CHILDREN TO DO HOMEWORK OR PLAY ON DEVICE

Do not allow computers, phones, tablets, or other devices to be used in private spaces. They should be centrally located, and screens should be visible to adults. For example, if you have a monitor attached to your machine it should be visible to anyone walking by when your child is doing homework or even play. When you allow your child to work alone on the computer in a room with no supervision, you ask for trouble.

As a former administrator, I have met with many parents who have been absolutely adamant that their child was online for hours the previous night doing homework. At the time I was able to pull statistics from the website the child was supposed to be logged into to do his work. When I showed the parent the statistics from the site, I demonstrated that the child was only logged in for two minutes, and the parent realized that "online" and "online in the correct site" are two totally different things. From then on, Jake had to do his homework at the kitchen table.

Bedtime for Phone/Device

Gaming systems should not be in bedrooms for a multitude of reasons. Children will be tempted to play all night, and if children play games online, you will not be able to recognize signs of predators. In addition, there needs to be a bedtime for every device in the home. What do I mean by this? I mean exactly what I said. The phone needs a bedtime. Many teenagers take their cell phones to bed with them. No way should this happen. I can hear it now…, "But Mom, it is my alarm." Please buy your child a traditional alarm clock. I suggest you have your child check in his or her device at a set time each night. This can be a central location for charging purposes. This will prevent late nights and make early school or church mornings much easier. This will also prevent late night texting or pictures from taking place when judgment may be decreased.

Many children will stay up late playing games on their devices or watching downloaded movies. Teenagers need their sleep for appropriate development. When you require that devices be docked at bedtime, there will be fewer distractions. Additionally, there is inconclusive evidence around the electromagnetic radiation cell phones emit and the potential damage to the brain. If your children are like most, they will sleep with the phone by their heads if allowed. It is best to limit this or turn the phone to airplane mode.

Establish Guidelines

Be involved with and establish guidelines for the sites your child or children are allowed to visit. For example, I would not allow my child to visit SecondLife. I have had many people tell me there are educational uses; however, each time I have entered, a flasher or stalker enters my page. I know how weird that sounds. This has happened regardless of my intent or the educational area I am in. You can easily search with your child and set parameters. You may also apply a filter to your home internet. There is software you can purchase or you can talk with your Internet Service Provider (ISP) about setting up firewalls to filter pornography. You should also be involved in social media sites, if you allow them. Approve who your children interact with on social media sites, and continue to have an open dialogue with them around their "friends."

It is a great idea to regularly visit your child's social media communities to see what information she has posted and discourage the use of web cams. Without resetting default passwords on your WiFi, anyone can access and see inside your home or capture images from your web cams. Also, images are geotagged by default. That means anyone can see where they were taken. Imagine, an innocent tagline like, "our new trampoline" attached to a picture of your new trampoline in your backyard on social media, with default GPS tagging that tells predators exactly where your child lives.

The bottom line is that you should make sure you discuss privacy with your child and that privacy settings are on. Side Note: *Please don't assume teachers are trained in this area because they aren't.*

If your child gets cyberbullied even though you may want to send a fiercely angry or threatening message back to the original sender, there are better ways to handle it. If the comments are online, the first step is to save the evidence. Then contact your ISP and ask them to remove the page where the threat or comments exist, if possible. If the bullying is on social media, save the evidence and then block the individual or groups who are doing the bullying. I'd suggest blocking the phone number if the comments are via text. Report cyberbullying to law enforcement if it includes:

- Threats of violence
- Child pornography or sending sexually explicit messages or photos

- Taking a photo or video of someone in a place where he or she would expect privacy
- Stalking and hate crimes

Some states consider cyberbullying criminal. If you have additional concerns, you should consult your specific state's anti-bullying laws and regulations. Stopbullying.gov provides this information in an easy to read chart, along with excellent facts and resources to support you if you are facing this situation.

If the individuals committing the bullying are from school, immediately notify school officials and ask them to assist you in dealing with the situation. Most importantly, discuss the comments with your child, and do NOT allow your child to respond. The comments will seem harsher than a comment made from a kid on the playground, since they are in writing. In actuality, they are no different. In guiding your child, you should advise the same way your great-grandfather would have coached your grandfather. I would imagine a conversation would go something like this:

"People who say ugly things about others usually do so because of their own insecurities. It is much easier to be mean when you are hiding behind a computer rather than facing someone. I feel sorry for them. There must be some circumstance we don't know about taking place in their homes. We should probably tell the school so they can investigate. I

know that doesn't make you feel better, but people don't lash out at others unless something is seriously wrong with them. It is easier to be mean to someone else than it is to accept that they really are the ones with a problem."

Obviously, if you feel something illegal has occurred, then you should inform law enforcement.

THE SMARTPHONE

You pay for it, so you should monitor it. Part of growing up is learning responsibility and how to manage priorities. Children are not mature enough to set their own limitations with phones. This is a responsibility they must learn. Check with your service provider regarding services that allow you to purchase additional services so that you can monitor usage, block certain numbers, control when your child's phone is on or off etc. There are also software packages that can be added to the phone to allow you to view all messages and images going in and out. Until your child learns the power and the risks involved with 24/7 access and communication, you, as the parent, need to monitor and supervise all digital interaction to ensure safety. The statistics are startling, and I've only shared a few of them.

I would also suggest a "no phone zone." Consider not allowing phones or devices at the dinner table. Conversation is still a needed skill. You need to spend time interacting with your child. If each of you texts or plays games constantly you will miss crucial opportunities to discuss the day's events or to communicate about meaningful events or activities. Keep an open dialogue. It is essential for emotional growth.

ONLINE SAFETY AT SCHOOL

Now that I have completely stressed you out, let's talk about what happens at school to protect your child while he or she is online. How you can find out school procedures and policies? And what your responsibilities are for digital interaction at school? After all, if you are in a school where your child is expected to bring his or her own device, then who is responsible for security? Or if your child is allowed to bring a device home from school, are you supposed to monitor it? This may all seem a bit overwhelming, especially now that I have gone through such startling statistics. Don't worry, I am going to walk through some of the details, so you will know the right questions to ask. As a matter of fact, you may be more prepared than the school is at this point since this is a new and emerging field.

I have suggested some general rules to establish a safer environment at home, but when your child goes to school, the suggested guidelines may be different. Regardless of the type of equipment the school uses, every school should have an Acceptable Use Policy (AUP) that you and your child should be asked to sign. If not, then you should ask to review it. This will outline the policy for internet technology. You may also ask to review the Online Safety Policy (OSP). It is likely that you and/or your child will be asked to sign these policies or other policies specific to the school school's particular digital learning initiative. Ideally, these policies should be posted on the school website, but if not, you may need to ask your child's school for them. I have provided some potential circumstances in which you would refer to the AUP or OSP.

- If your child is allowed to use a device from home such as a tablet or phone, review the documents carefully to determine who is liable if the device is stolen at school.

- Will you be responsible for providing mobile data usage or will your child be allowed to log onto the school's wireless network? This is also a security question. On the school's network the school's firewall will be in place, which will include security. Are you responsible for monitoring security during school hours on your child's device?

- If cyber bullying takes place during school hours, even if the device is your child's personal machine, then will the school be held responsible?

All of these questions and concerns should be addressed in the Acceptable Use Policy (AUP) and/or Online Safety Policy (OSP). However, please remember this is still a new field, so you may need to specifically ask if you have concerns about topics that are not outlined or documented in the policy or procedure provided by the school. These same questions are applicable whether your child is using a device provided by the school OR if your child is completing a homework assignment online required by the teacher. Let me give you an example:

> *If Mr. Blackwell requires students to post a response to a question in a blog for homework, even if he requires it to be completed at home on personal devices, since he required it, will he be monitoring the blog for inappropriate comments?*

> *If the assignment is required, then of course he should be monitoring it. Since it is a required assignment, it should only be taking place in a secure and safe location, as should be indicated in the AUP and/or OSP.*

So far, we have talked about hardware and other people's children. What if you are concerned about an assignment? Teachers generally have good intentions, but what if you don't particularly want your child researching adultery online when she reads *The Scarlet Letter*? Or what if there is a sensitive family situation that your child may discover if he researches family history? Obviously, your child's teacher cannot be aware of all circumstances, nor can he or she know your personal values. That being said, there is nothing wrong with asking for an alternative assignment.

Please see the sample emails in the previous chapter for ideas of how to communicate your concern(s). Certainly, depending on the nature of the assignment and the level of detail you want to disclose, this type of request may be handled better over the telephone or in person.

Speaking of communicating with the teacher, what if your child insists that he was on Facetime last night until 2 am because he was working on a group project? First, let's consider the guidelines I suggested previously. If the use of electronic devices is in a public place in your home, then you will know what is being discussed on Facetime, and you will be able to redirect the conversation to keep the children on task if, in fact, the topic of conversation is school related. Therefore, this group activity probably wouldn't have lasted until 2 am since you would have been able to keep the children focused and on task.

Hopefully the teacher posted details of the assignment on her webpage or online class calendar. If you cannot verify the assignment by any digital means, then, be sure to contact the teacher by email or phone to verify before you ground your child. Facetime or Skype is actually a great way to collaborate. However, if the activity was school related, it sounds like the children involved need some help with time management. My guess is that the conversation lasted until 2 am because they were distracted and discussed the attire for the prom rather than or in addition to their senior project.

Remember that you can block sites or set your privacy settings to prevent specific sites from being available. As a matter of fact, you can disable or restrict Facetime through the settings app if you'd like. For example, your child may be distracted with incoming Facetime requests when working on digital assignments. In this situation, it may be best to restrict Facetime until homework is complete. There are many software programs or even router-based programs for parents to implement to ensure safety for children. There are even safe search engines designed for kids and younger learners: Kiddle™, DuckDuckGo™, and GoGoGooligans™ to name a few.

STUDENT PRIVACY

Let's talk about why passwords and user identifications, among other methods for data protection, are so important. We have a regulation in the United States to protect student privacy called Family Education Rights and Privacy Act (FERPA). I'm sure you have heard a lot about protecting sensitive data online for yourself, and you may have your own concerns about your child's data being available online. As a result, I'm going to go into a bit of detail, so you will be informed and can make sure your child's sensitive information is being protected, not only at school but also at home. This is extremely important.

Under the "Protection of Pupil Rights Amendment," (PPRA), as a parent, you have the right to opt out of any activity that would expose any "Personally Identifiable Information" (PII) for your child. Personally, identifiable information contains direct identifiers such as family members' names or student names and indirect identifiers such as date of birth, place of birth or mother's maiden name. So, under PPRA, if your child is taking a digital course that requires PII, then you can request that he or she be given the course in paper format instead. This would obviously be because you are concerned that personally identifiable information would be accessed by the wrong person or organization online. In context, an example of this may be that you are afraid an abusive parent could discover the whereabouts of your child by tracking him down online or that you are afraid his social security number would be stolen by a thief. These are, of course, extreme examples, but I use them to illustrate the point.

You should be aware that, under FERPA, the school has the right to release directory information, which is information such as your child's name, address, telephone listing, email, date, place of birth, pictures, weight and height of athletes, degrees, and awards. This is why identifiable information is listed in yearbooks and athletic or music programs. However, under PPRA, since this is Personally Identifiable Information, you, as a parent, have the right to opt out by requesting that the school not include or identify your child, if you have a concern.

This is all extremely important information to know, especially when a school begins to explore the digital environment. Your child's school may contract with a third-party provider to purchase curriculum or to build a webpage. In some cases, the school district has the right to provide your child's data, if it is a service the school would normally provide. In other cases, you have to give permission if PII is given to the third-party provider.

Let me give you an example. We have heard great things about Khan Academy, an online or digital provider of curriculum. Many schools use their math content, for example. They have been featured on 20/20, Nightline... you name it, but an investigation by *Edweek*, and educational journal, in 2014 found that they "are essentially enabling third parties to gather unlimited information about users and disclaiming any responsibility." (Scrutinizing data policies of Edmodo, Khan, and Pearson, 2014, p. 1) This is a bit alarming since parental permission isn't requested.

ONLINE ASSESSMENTS

While I am on the topic of data collection, the most obvious example of this topic is the controversial standards and assessment movement we currently face. I'm sure you have heard of some of the concerns with Common Core and national electronic testing. There is an automatic association between testing and the standards, so let me clarify. The standards are one initiative, and the testing is another. It seems to make sense to me that every child in America be held accountable for the same standards or knowledge regardless of which state he or she lives in. In other words, if you live in Florida and get transferred to Alabama for work, your 3rd grader will be studying the same thing in 3rd grade in Alabama as he was in Florida. Believe it or not, prior to Common Core standards, children in different states, counties, and even schools did not study the same things in the same grades. What was taught in each grade could have been drastically different. My intent is not to debate the quality of the standards, just to explain the concept, which seems to make sense and is really where the idea started.

Online testing is when we begin to worry about security of our children's data. We have already discussed why Gen Z needs digital literacy and exposure. Can you imagine grading multiple choice tests for every student in the U.S.? Of course not, so digital testing makes sense from that perspective. However, who is ensuring that their privacy is protected? Statistical models and prediction instruments can be amazingly accurate. Who will have our children's testing data in their hands? Who is monitoring their Personally Identifiable Information (PII)? These are all concerns with internet safety. What will be done with all of these test scores? As a parent, under The Protection of Pupil Rights Amendment (PPRA), you have the right to insert yourself into this dialogue. You should be the strongest advocate for your child. I encourage you to become involved in these conversations and to be informed simply from a data awareness standpoint.

Many states modified legislation to accommodate needs for the Common Core standards and for the testing to measure accountability during the 2013 and 2014 sessions (Common Core standards initiative: preparing America's students for college and career, 2018). The creation of an infrastructure capable to digitally test every student in the United States is an expensive and complicated undertaking. As of 2019, some states are still not able to successfully test students digitally. I encourage every parent to be involved at the local level, at the least, to learn how these changes impact their children. I also encourage you to dialogue with your child's teachers to make sure you understand the testing data. It can be insightful information to provide a window into your child's strengths and areas for growth. Used appropriately and securely, the data can be a wonderful tool for educators. It is your responsibility as a parent to monitor and advocate for security and appropriateness in the use of your child's data.

STUDENT STORY

While the anonymity of being behind a computer screen can certainly bring out the worst in some children, it is also a great way to bring out the best in some children. In rural area of the country, a young man, who I will call

Jeff, was described as being severely overweight, having a bad complexion, and coming from a poor family. Jeff had been so truant from school that he was behind five classes and would not be able to graduate with his peers. In a last-ditch effort to help him graduate, the school enrolled him in online classes. Because the young man lived in a poor, rural farm community, he did not have internet at home, so he had to come to the school to use the computer lab for his online classes. In the online classes, neither the teacher nor other students could see his physical appearance, and Jeff's participation soared.

He began coming to school every day, (even though he literally had holes in the bottoms of his shoes) because this was his only way to access his online classes. He loved online learning. Nobody made fun of him, and he wasn't self-conscious since nobody could see him. His experience taking online classes showed the administration at the school that he had potential for leadership, so they gave him responsibilities in the computer lab, which furthered his growing confidence and encouraged his attendance. Jeff was able to make up the five classes he was behind, and he graduated with a regular diploma, along with the experience of being a lab leader. Had he not been enrolled in the online classes, Jeff would likely not have graduated, nor would his leadership potential have been discovered.

CHAPTER 7
PROBLEM SOLVING: ALL CHILDREN HAVE UNIQUE NEEDS

Yeah, yeah, I know the type. You have a sticker on your car saying that your child made the honor roll. I can't say much. When my daughter took her first step, I looked breathlessly to see if she did it before she was "supposed to," according to "experts."

We all know that every child is special, especially according to his mother. However, in reality, there are times when special needs arise where blended or online courses are a perfect solution for some children. It is hard to create an exhaustive list because there are so many circumstances where digital education is a better fit for a child than traditional, face-to-face education, but some might be:

- A gifted student may need a more advanced class than others, so she will be challenged. Unfortunately, all schools cannot offer exactly what every child needs since all children are different.

- Perhaps the middle school doesn't offer the class a transfer student needs.

- Possibly the student needs access to extra practice activities.

- The student may need to complete partial work to make up credit.

- The student may need to retake a course over summer for athletic eligibility.

- Maybe the young adult lacked one class to earn a diploma yet opted for a GED. After further consideration, he decided to make up the class and get a diploma instead thanks to online flexibility.

- Perhaps the traditional school doesn't have a certified teacher for the class a child wants to take but can get one online.

- The school may not have science materials, so it uses online simulations instead of live labs.

- Perhaps the classroom is flipped.

- Albeit unfortunate, maybe there is school bullying taking place.

- Maybe a parent wants faith-based education options rather than traditional options a school can offer.

- The student may want to remain in the socially appropriate environment but needs less difficult academic work.

- The student may be hospitalized but be well enough to complete schoolwork online.

- The student may need to make up work from several absences.

- The school may have digital textbooks.

- Maybe the child has anxiety and becomes physically ill when in school.

Depending on your child's interests and needs there are specific details you will want to verify as you pursue this opportunity. The most common concerns I hear from parents are around course fees and NCAA, so I will begin with those.

COURSE FEES
Exceptional Education/Gifted

If your child has an Individualized Education Plan (IEP), because he has special needs, you have some options when it comes to paying for online course that others may not have. It is important that you understand your rights and are vocal in being the advocate for your child.

If you have explored options that have not been successful in the public education system, or if you simply think your child would do well in an online class, find out if your school or school district offers online classes. Then begin working with the exceptional education department to have the digital option written into the IEP. If the program is written into the IEP, 504 plan, or even Behavior Intervention Plan (BIP), then the fees for online course are paid, if the district charges. Most of the examples I listed above are legitimate uses of public funding, except for faith-based education preferences, of course.

This approach may allow you access to additional funding. For example, if your child struggled during math throughout the school year, then ask that he take an online course for remediation or additional help in your IEP meeting. If your child is gifted, and you feel an additional course would better challenge him or her, or if a foreign language that isn't offered at the school might support his or her goals, ask that one be included in the IEP. This may create opportunities for the school to use funding to pay for the course(s). The school can then assist you with finding a reputable digital or online course and teacher if the district doesn't have an online provider already.

For those of you who don't know to what I'm referring with an IEP, then it means that your child doesn't receive special services from the school. So, you may not be eligible for this type of funding. Don't completely discount the idea that funding might be available if tuition is required for an online course, though. If you receive any special services such as free or reduced lunch there may be scholarship programs or funds for summer school available. Even if your child doesn't have an IEP, many state's 529 plans will allow you to pay for online courses, even if your child is homeschooled.

I always suggest parents ask. If your child *needs* a class that the school does *not* offer, then it is usually the school's responsibility to pay for the course online. Let me give you an example.

In eighth grade, Annabelle had completed all the higher-level math the middle school offered. In the past, the middle school would pay a bus to take students in her situation to the high school to take high school-level math.

This was nerve wracking for Annabelle, not to mention her mother. With online courses, it was more economical for Annabelle to go to the middle school library and take her class online. With technology, she can digitally sign into the high school class and even participate and interact with the teacher. This saves a considerable amount of money and trauma.

If this is not an option, there are plenty of credible online courses available, where the school can enroll Annabelle. It is the school's responsibility to ensure the courses are credible and appropriate for Annabelle's transcript.

A different scenario, though, is if your child is like many teenagers…lazy. Did I say that? Let me give you an example.

Rik goofed off and skipped many of his 11th grade English classes. As a matter of fact, he depended on his girlfriend to do most of his work. As a result, he did not pass the class. His parents were, of course, shocked, and demanded he go to summer school. Sadly, they had already scheduled their vacation, which was right in the middle of June.

Fortunately, the school offered an alternative of online summer school. Rik was able to retake his 11th grade English online. As long as he logged into his class, interacted with his teacher and peers, and submitted his work on schedule, he only had to come to the school in person for the final exam. Since failing the class was his own fault, he or his parents had to foot the bill.

Many schools, if policy allows, offer ways that Rik could have prevented going to summer school altogether through something called credit recovery. In these programs, students are allowed to make up failing work by completing the work again in digital forms. Typically, schools average the new grade with the old grade for the individual units, but this policy varies by district and state. This allows students to successfully complete work as they go, so they don't wind up with a failing grade at the end of the course. These programs may be offered after school, in summer, during homeroom programs or on Saturdays.

Another example that can sometimes be tricky is something Nanny McPhee teaches us. If a student wants to take an online course, but doesn't need an online course, then the school is not required to pay. Previously I said that the school should pay if the school doesn't offer a course required for a student. Let me give you an example of how this applies.

> *Annabelle, the overachieving student described previously, wanted to take Mandarin Chinese, but her school didn't offer it. The school did offer Spanish I and II. A two-year sequence of a foreign language is required for college entrance.*

Quiz time! Should the school pay for Annabelle to take Mandarin Chinese online? The answer is no. The school offered the requirement. It just wasn't in the language in which Annabelle was interested. If the school approved, then Annabelle's parents may have paid for the online course. If I were Annabelle's parent, I would have requested confirmation in writing prior to registering for the class. Specifically, the confirmation should state that the credit would be accepted towards graduation for any digital classes I, as a parent, paid.

Interestingly, even if your child doesn't have an IEP, many state's 529 plans will allow you to use funds to pay for online courses, even if your child is homeschooled. Especially, in high school, if your child aspires to be in the top 10%, Salutatorian or Valedictorian, please request these policies and how online courses impact these rankings before signing up for one. In some states, if a child needs to retake a course in order to improve his grade point average for a lottery scholarship he can do this by paying to retake a course online. If the course cost $500, and it allows a senior to now qualify for 120 hours of college tuition, is it worth it? You do the math!

NCAA

Recently, I met an obsessed little league parent, who said his nine-year-old was going to play professional football. Are you done laughing? As a former college athlete, I just shake my head at some of the obsessed little league parents. Nonetheless, I have worked in several roles ensuring student-athletes are eligible to play collegiate sports. As a former high school coach and athletic director, I completed eligibility paperwork for the NCAA. As an administrator in digital programs, I have been responsible for ensuring digital coursework meets NCAA guidelines and that organizations have followed all rules for NCAA approval to certify enrolled student-athletes meet academic guidelines to maintain eligibility for the NCAA clearinghouse.

As someone who personally went through the clearinghouse as a student-athlete, I recognize the emotional stake involved in remaining conscientious of the NCAA's expectations for academic eligibility for student-athletes, parents, coaches, and administrators.

The NCAA's expectations, as I will describe, are primarily around fully digital or online courses and not necessarily blended courses. However, this topic is often misunderstood, and it is so important that I am going to focus in depth on it. I sincerely feel that we, as parents, should be the strongest advocates for our children. I do not want your child redshirted the first four games of his or her freshman season while the high school works on paperwork with the NCAA because it did not go through the approval process for a course your child took in 12th grade because the school didn't have a certified teacher in pre-calculus, for example, or because the school wasn't aware of the NCAA approval process.

As far as eligibility for college sports, there is nothing wrong with your child taking an online or blended class, as long as the correct paperwork is filed, and the course is from a credible program that has been approved by the NCAA. As a matter of fact, the experience of participating in digital content or taking a class online is a good one for your child. He or she will be well-prepared for this opportunity at the collegiate level. I intend to go into detail around "credible" and what this looks like to the NCAA.

When going through the clearinghouse for eligibility, the NCAA reviews your child's transcript. The transcript reflects all the courses your child has taken for high school credit. Digital learning, which can take on different models such as 1:1, flipped, or blended (defined in Chapter 2) is a teaching method or style that a teacher chooses to use in the traditional classroom, so there is no differentiation on a transcript. For example, if the teacher chooses to have the students go to a website to read a short story rather than use a book or if a teacher chooses to have the students interact with an electronic science lab rather than physically go to the lab and smell formaldehyde, there is no need to make a note of it on the transcript. Either way, the students are reporting to a physical classroom. Great teachers obviously need creativity and freedom to teach the way they find best in their own classrooms.

However, the NCAA will be wary of your child's transcripts if they reflect online, distance learning, correspondence, or software-based credit recovery courses. In some instances, there have been cases when student-athletes have attempted to pay fees to enroll in particularly easy courses just so they get a passing grade to remain eligible to play college sports. It seems the tricksters find the easiest way to do this in online or via distance-learning courses. I know you are shocked that kids looked for the easy way out. While our society is crazed with athletics, the primary purpose of school is academics, and there is no replacement for passing grades that students work hard to earn.

Because of scams to keep student-athletes eligible with phony courses, the NCAA will investigate to make sure that online courses are academic and comparable to what is truly offered in the traditional classroom. Otherwise, student-athletes will miss learning important skills and may be set up for failure. Can you imagine if you paid a fee for a passing grade, but your child never learned senior English? What happens when he or she is a freshman trying to pass College Composition?

In order to help protect your child and make sure that online and distance learning service providers provide the services needed, the NCAA requires that organizations offering online and distance courses include access to a qualified teacher. In other words, if your child needs to retake a class to be eligible, you won't pay a fee and then be hung out to dry with no human being to ask for help. A diploma mill won't help prepare your child for college. There may be times when your child actually needs a teacher to explain concepts. I know I certainly couldn't help my niece with Physics, even though I have a doctorate in learning.

It is important to know that the NCAA requires any digital courses you or the school signs your child up for to have a defined period of time, so there has to be a solid begin date and end date. Basically, there has to be a standard timeline, a course name, rigor, and live teacher associated with the course (like when we went to school!). Imagine that. This really doesn't sound like much more than common sense. You'd be surprised at the number of online course providers who will try to take your money and promise that your child will be eligible if he or she takes their courses. Unfortunately, some parents don't find out until the first two-a-day practice when their child's coach is making many, many phone calls to try and solve the problem.

Speaking of solving problems, let's talk about credit recovery. It is a bit of a different animal. Some schools offer it, and others don't. Usually states or school districts will have a policy concerning credit recovery. In it, districts or schools allow students to retake a course or portion of a course and then average the new grade with the old grade to create a combined new grade. Policy usually dictates how high this grade can be, and it may be different in each state or district. Let me give you an example by talking about James:

> *James was an excellent running back in high school, and he had opportunities to play DII football in college. However, he struggled in Spanish, which is required for a college preparatory diploma. His*

school had a credit recovery program, where he spent lots of time. Even though he didn't learn much more than to count to ten in Spanish, say "hola," and maybe a few Spanish cuss words, he was able to pass the course through credit recovery because he worked very hard.

During the traditional school day he'd go to Spanish class. On Tuesday, for example, he failed a unit test on the seasons with a 58. He spent the next week after school, every day, in credit recovery, where he did additional practice activities in an online credit recovery course. At the end of the week he retook the unit test on the seasons, where he scored an 89. The average of the two test grades was a 73, but the school policy didn't allow him to score higher than a 70 on any credit recovery grade. The credit recovery work, though, allowed him a passing score on the unit, and the 70 replaced his original 58.

As far as the NCAA is concerned, as long as the school follows its credit recovery policy, and there is consistency among athletes and non-athletes within the policy, then credit recovery is perfectly acceptable. Credit recovery courses are required to be noted on your child's transcript by the NCAA, and just as in James' case, they should be equivalent to the rigor he received in the traditional classroom.

So now that I've made you completely nervous, what do you do when your child needs to make up a course? Or what if the school only offers online summer school? Relax. The hard work is really the responsibility of the school. You just need to be informed and ask the right questions. You know enough now to see red flags. Follow the guidelines I have outlined above. Ask the guidance counselor if the NCAA has approved the course(s), and if the course seems too easy, then it probably is. Remember, it is your job to be your child's advocate. If your child just logs in and clicks buttons for credit without ever reading or interacting with a teacher or taking a quiz or test, then something is probably a little fishy.

The best thing you can do is check to see if the NCAA has approved the course. Oh yes, accountability exists. Go to the NCAA Eligibility Center's Website at www. eligibilitycenter.org. If you'd prefer or have questions that the school guidance counselor cannot answer, then you can contact the NCAA Eligibility Center at 1-877-262-1492.

GENERAL INFORMATION

This is all way too serious for me. I just want a resource for my child on breaks and in the summer to help improve some skills or to get a jump start. Does this mean I should pay for software? Not in most cases. Most states have end-of-course testing. Because of this, you should be able to ask your teacher for your child's academic strengths and weaknesses based on test scores. During the school year it is likely that your child's teacher conducts a type of testing called a benchmark or benchmarking. This identifies areas for growth and strength, as the benchmark tests align to the end-of-course test as the school year progresses. I'd suggest aligning any work from home you do to classroom weaknesses. For example, if my child showed a weakness in mastering standards associated with multiplying fractions I'd then go to Google and type in "practice multiplying fractions." I'd search until I found a FREE site or sites that covered the topic well and had sufficient practice. I discussed how to find credible sites in Chapter 3, so you may want to review it when you get a chance.

I would follow this same method if my child was out of school for a few weeks and needed to make up work. What if I have a stack of make-up assignments to work through with my child, and I don't even know how to do some of it? Trust me. The internet can be your friend. Do not pay for sites. Many, many teachers have worked hard to put good, resourceful sites online for students, other teachers, and parents. Even though you may not be a teacher, if there are lesson plans online, you can read them for information or ideas on how to help your child with the topic.

Other times when you may want to use the internet as an academic supplement may include:

- If you have a trip planned, but you are still concerned about your child's academics. Maybe your child has to write an essay. There are sites to help teach him about the major components of an essay.

- Is it time for the Science Fair? Hello. Who likes coming up with all those ideas for the Science Fair? I say find a great idea online and go for it! Did someone say Pinterest? There are some very nice parents who have "been there, done that." Fortunately, they did win the medal, and they have placed their ideas online to help you survive your busy life and parenting!

STUDENT STORY

Elaine's parents were killed in a car accident during her junior year in high school. She continued to attend school while working a full-time job to support herself and her younger sibling. She attended a traditional school that offered credit recovery online as well as full-time online courses. Because of the tragedy her junior year, Elaine failed her second semester courses. Through online credit recovery she was able to earn back her credits. During her senior year, she took two classes online and two classes in person. This flexibility allowed her to continue working and graduate with a diploma.

CHAPTER 8
LEARNING IS FUN?

BADGES

Do you think your child is missing out on some experiences you had as a child in school? In gaming or digital curriculum, when educators provide an incentive like you may have received with a scratch and sniff sticker, it is called badging. The concept is the same as a classroom teacher giving you a sticker, candy, or allowing you to leave five minutes early. You remember those days. You do something correct or great, and you get rewarded with an incentive. We received a sticker that we scratched to release a scent, and our children receive badges or tokens that ultimately represent accomplishments.

Often, the goal is to collect as many badges or tokens as they can, to show status, or to level up, and to show how accomplished they are as players/learners. It can be a lot like a game, so you may have heard it called gamification of learning. It is important that, as a parent of a Generation Z child, who is participating in digital learning, that you fully understand digital badging. Otherwise, you just might not be cool, and I wouldn't want that.

We all know the idea behind the badges the Boy and Girl Scouts have had for years. They are symbols of accomplishment. Digital badges/tokens are a similar concept, except they are intended to bridge academic and social behaviors by using game-like motivation. Think about it. If your child is learning through gamification and earns a badge, then he is rewarded and motivated to continue playing and thus learning. Success has been communicated to others and to your child; your child has been motivated because the great work has been reinforced. Oh…and all this was done while learning by using what educators call gamification.

Gamification is another way that educators bridge the gap between entertainment and education. Children now are born digital natives. Badges are not only used as rewards, but they are also used for goal setting; both of which encourage positive behavior in the digital age. Badges and tokens can represent skills or even awards, similar to a portfolio. Depending on the model the school has set up, students may even be able to earn certifications by way of badges or tokens or as actual credentials. For high-school age children, these could be equivalent to industry certifications. Beyond the concept of a sticker, so to speak, or a more traditional portfolio, badges and tokens also have real-world applications, where when verified or awarded by a third party, are transferable in a technology called blockchain.

BLOCKCHAIN

Blockchain serves as a digital ledger, and it is currently one of the most secure ways to store our personal data. Individuals have a key or password, and they control who can see or award credentials to their personal profile. Typically, you have what is called a "wallet," where you can access or show others the credentials or data you have on your blockchain. Currently when employers award or verify training credentials to the blockchain of a specific employee, the employee accepts them, and the credentials transfer or stay with the employee the remainder of his working career, regardless of the company. Imagine going to a job interview, opening your "wallet" or app, and showing all the trainings you have had throughout your career.

Similarly, education institutions can award transcript data, badges, awards, service hours, and/or work-force readiness certificates to the blockchain. Completing training(s) in soft skills, something current employers see as a great need for potential candidates, could even be on a student's blockchain. Assessment companies are exploring adding test scores to blockchain. Sending test scores to universities is time consuming and has a cost. If your child's test scores lived on his blockchain, then there would be no need to request documentation. Your child would already have it! Once credentials are verified by the awarding institution and accepted by the student (and/or parent if the student is under 18), they would stay on the student's permanent digital ledger or digital file as evidence of attaining a skill, diploma, score, degree or certification for others to see, much like a digital transcript or digital resume. I don't know if you went back to school as an adult, but having to request transcripts, especially if you have gone to multiple colleges or universities, is no fun. The main difference in what I described with blockchain technology is that the learner is the center and in control. In the past, the learner has been at the behest of the institution. This learner-centric design of awarding historical data is just one model of how digital innovations are driving education to evolve into a more student-centered personalized ecosystem.

Don't get me wrong, the Kool-Aid isn't for everyone. There is criticism that badges are awarded to children for behaviors they should be doing anyway, which creates a false sense of accomplishment or rewards behavior that should be taking place without the need for reward. This is true, but I'm going to discuss one-way badging is used in blended and online learning through competency-based learning (See

Chapter 3). Both of these topics are fairly new, hot topics, so you may have already experienced them, or they may be headed your way.

In a traditional work environment, job titles are a way to know skill levels. This is also a form of badging. For example, if I work in a plant, I know that the MIG Welder has a different skillset than the TIG Welder. I also know that a Clerk has a different skillset than an Administrative Assistant. If I were to break down all the skills necessary to perform each of the previously mentioned jobs, I'd have a list of skills or competencies. Education is much the same. There is a list of competencies or skills that students must master in order to pass each grade. Competency-based instruction is a fancy way of saying each student works at his own pace with the opportunity to test out of skills he may already have. By demonstrating mastery, he only has to focus on new skills he may not know yet.

In a traditional classroom, with textbooks and papers to grade, it is very difficult for a teacher to manage every individual student's capability in every standard. Imagine having to know and determine 200+ students' strengths and weakness in over 100 areas and how those shape and grow daily. Oh, and by the way, you have your own family to take care of as well. With the help of technology, however, a student's knowledge can be assessed and monitored, and this measurement can be incorporated into blended and/ or online learning. This allows the teacher to know each student's skills by way of a game or test the student performs on the computer. Based on individualized data provided by the software, a teacher can automatically measure which competencies students have already mastered. Then the teacher can focus on teaching rather than assessing. Why bore your child with stuff he already knows? Let's award him a badge for already mastering those skills. Then we can challenge him with some harder work and set some goals that are specific to his personal academic needs and interests.

Did you see how I brought the badging and the competency together there? You get badges for what you master. Your reward for mastering work is a badge, and your goal is to master all competencies thus earning more badges. This is a great way to build your child's self-esteem. He isn't competing with classmates. He is only competing with his individualized goals, and mastery is set at his own level of accomplishment. In other words, he won't compare himself to other children like in a large traditional classroom. The technology actually allows teachers to work with the children one-on-one while they work at their individual paces.

Here is where it starts to get really fun! Some programs even allow you to stack credentials for badging. Let's go back to the Clerk vs. the Administrative Assistant example. Both have clerical skills. We know that the Administrative Assistant and the Clerk have some of the same skills, so, we can assume they'd have some of the same badges. We can call those Level 1 badges, for the sake of explanation. To continue on to be an Administrative Assistant, though, there are additional skills to be learned or advanced clerical skills. Those are Level 2 skills. So, the Administrative Assistant would have stacked credentials with both Level 1 and 2 badges; whereas the Clerk may only have Level 1 badges. An Executive Assistant, on the other hand, probably demonstrated competency in Levels 1, 2, and 3. You can imagine how this applies with writing skills or math skills as students advance grades.

RECAP

We started this book with the basics. Your child brought home assignments on the computer for homework rather than work in a textbook, and look how far we've come. Now you are already to the point of understanding competency-based learning and individualized instruction, where schools use technology that allows the teacher to be a facilitator rather than the sage on the stage.

Gone are the days where the teacher does what educators call "whole group instruction," or where the teacher is the sage on the stage. In the traditional model the teacher lectures all the students on the same skill or topic, regardless of their individual ability or understanding. This probably is something you are familiar with from your days in school. "Class, please turn to page 143 and lets all read together."

All kids are expected to be ready for the skill or all kids are expected to be at the same level, regardless of whether they are advanced or behind, which means they may be bored and even misbehave.

Of course, there are exceptions to this example, and their may have been when you were a student with respect to inclusion classrooms, but that isn't to what I'm referring. In an inclusion classroom, students who are in the exceptional education program may not be distinguishable from regular education students. Although, by law, these students may have modifications for the amount or type of work they are assigned. This is because students with special needs have what is called an Individualized Education Plan (IEP), and by law the modifications in the IEP must be followed. These students have had extensive testing to determine their needs and the type of support that will help them be more successful in the classroom.

With technology, the computer can adapt or recognize patterns in all learner responses. Essentially, the computer notes, Elizabeth is responding like these 100 other students, so she must need this style question next. This is adaptive learning. The more questions Elizabeth answers, and the more students who participate in the software, the more exact the software gets in accurately providing the learning Elizabeth needs. This is why it is called adaptive software, and this is significantly better at diagnosing Elizabeth's learning trends than one teacher's brain in a classroom of 30 students when the teacher is also trying to manage taking up money for the field trip, classroom management, announcements, teaching low-level and high-level students, attendance reports, etc. Ack! As I write this, I also remember that teachers are woefully underpaid.

What this "adaptive" software does, is provides detailed data to the teacher for her to see Elizabeth's exact strengths and weaknesses. It is almost like peeking into Elizabeth's brain. Then the teacher can reteach or create small groups based on where students show strengths or weaknesses. It is as if every student has an individualized learning plan. One of the greatest values to students completing their work in digital curriculum is the data that is collected by the software on the backend, when it is appropriate, as we discussed in Chapter 2. Learner data, when interpreted correctly, can be the best resource for you and the teacher because it allows you to diagnose problems and recognize areas for growth for your child. You can meet the child exactly where she is academically. There is no need to teach to the middle or to the top—the guesswork is gone.

So, why aren't all schools doing this? In order to teach using this method, schools need equipment and teachers who are trained specifically in competency-based education. Teachers and administrators are just beginning to see how this works, and badging is really a new concept in education. As you can imagine, schools need money to train teachers and buy software, so they can implement more of this.

However, if your child is currently in a blended class, I'm sure there are tidbits of this happening, and it won't be long before there are more.

Over six million US college students, mostly undergraduates, took an online class in 2016, which was an increase of 5.6% from the year prior, more than triple the number from the previous three years. In public universities almost two-thirds of students enroll in online courses (Friedman, 2018). Yowzers! If your child is college-bound, I'd definitely suggest taking an online class just to prepare for college. Currently Alabama, Arkansas, Florida, Michigan, and Virginia all require students to take an online class in order to graduate.

If you are still skeptical about digital education, perhaps you should consider that "Over 80% of Fortune 500 companies, like Target and Wal-Mart, require online job applications. In the next decade, it is estimated that nearly 80% of jobs will require digital skills" (Usdan & Almasy, 2012).

Furthermore, a leading researcher in digital education, Clayton Christenson, predicted that by 2019, 50% of education in the US would be offered online, which is a good thing, given the need for digital literacy to compete in the 21st century job market (Christensen, Johnson, & Horn, 2008). So, when your child's teacher includes digital resources in homework or classwork assignments, using methods that are different than the way you or I learned, while it is easy to get frustrated, just remember that teachers are preparing your child or children to be successful adults. By supporting their efforts, we can educate our children for a global economy.

It is our duty as parents to be involved in our children's education and to educate ourselves so that we can serve as their advocates to ensure that they are receiving the quality education they need to be successful global citizens. When your children were toddlers you made sure the environments they played in were safe, and for toddlers, playing is a form of constant learning. Think of your engagement in their digital environment in the same way as you when you bought and inserted plastic covers on all of your outlets for your first child. The need to ensure our children are safe doesn't go away when they are online or in bigger bodies, even if they think so. In order for your children to be safe online and truly experience the educational benefits technology can provide, you have to be just as engaged as their teachers, if not more.

We must also stretch our own skills, as you may have when reading this book, in order to ensure their safety in an ever-expanding digital world. Schools are now reaching out to us, as parents, by way of digital communications such as Remind and ClassDoJo, to name a few, and a 2017 study by Columbia University found a 28% increase in student attendance and a 12% reduction in course failures when teacher's sent weekly digital communications to parents that included current grade, missing assignments, and attendance with such low-cost apps (Bergman & Chan, 2019). Other schools are using apps like SeeSaw, which allow students to take a picture or video of what they are doing in class and add audio. With the teacher's permission, the student can send the file to a parent during class, and the parent can respond with questions. The data demonstrates how parental engagement with the tools technology provides improves the educational experience. The question isn't whether your child is ready for a digital education. The question is are you ready?

ABOUT THE AUTHOR

With over fifteen years of leadership experience in digital education, Dr. Wendy Oliver has worked with ten states, focusing her consulting work on implementing innovative learning models and creating life-long learning experiences. Throughout her career, which began as a teacher, Wendy has had the opportunity to develop and pioneer district and state-wide digital learning programs, beginning in The State of Tennessee. She also served as the Chief Learning Architect for Arizona State University's digital 9-12 charter school.

Wendy created Oliver's Frameworks for Blended and Online Instruction, and subsequent software that allows teachers to self-assess their educational knowledge in each respective environment, where they also receive credentialed, personalized, professional development pathways.

Dr. Oliver now focuses her energy at the national level working on best practices in digital education and consulting with educators in order to build successful digital learning models. Most recently she co-led the rewrite of the national online teaching standards, and served on the national leadership team to rewrite the standards for designing quality online courses.

As someone who loves to learn, no matter which hat she's wearing, her goal is simple—to empower learners.

www.DrWendyOliver.com

@oliver_dr

APPENDIX A
HOW TO DELETE PASSWORDS FROM PUBLIC COMPUTERS

Internet Explorer

1. **Open** the browser.
2. Press the **Tools** icon located on the **top-right browser's corner**.
3. Choose **Internet Options** from the menu.
4. Click the **Content** tab available between **Privacy** and **Connections** tabs.
5. Search for **AutoComplete** options and press the **Settings** button.
6. Click the **Delete AutoComplete history** button.
7. Tick the **checkbox** next to **Password** and any other data you wish to erase.
8. Select **Delete**.
9. Click **OK** twice to **close** the previously opened windows.

Safari

1. Go to the **Safari** menu.
2. Choose **Preferences**.
3. Search for the **AutoFill** tab.

4. Press the **Edit** button for both **Usernames and Passwords**.
5. **Select entries** you wish to erase and press Delete.
6. Close the **Preferences** window.

Mozilla Firefox

1. **Launch** the browser.
2. Press the **menu** button.
3. Select **Options** and go to the **Privacy & Security** tab.
4. Find the **Forms & Passwords** option.
5. Click the **Saved Logins** option available below the **Exceptions** button.
6. Press Remove All to erase all saved passwords at once or select separate passwords and click Remove.
7. Press Close to finish.

Google Chrome

1. Open **Google Chrome**.
2. Click the **menu** icon available on the **top-right corner**.
3. Press **Settings**.
4. If no user is signed in the first group of options should be titled **Person 1**; otherwise, it might show **a particular username**.
5. Select the **Passwords** tab and look for **Saved Passwords**.
6. **Locate the password** you wish to erase.

7. Click the **More Actions** icon (**three dots**) on the right side.

8. Select **Remove** and the password will be deleted.

9. **Close** the password settings **tab**.

APPENDIX B
EXAMPLE ACCEPTABLE USE POLICY (AUP) FROM BOSTON PUBLIC SCHOOLS

In order to review an acceptable use policy, use your smart device to scan the QR code below or go to:

www.bostonpublicschools.org/domain/2330

APPENDIX C
EXAMPLE/TEMPLATE INTERNET SAFETY POLICY PROVIDED BY ERATE

In order to access an example Internet safety policy, use your smart device to scan the following QR code or go to:

www.e-ratecentral.com/Portals/0/DocFiles/files/cipa/
cipa_policy_sample.pdf

APPENDIX D
HELPFUL WEBSITES BY SUBJECT

Anatomy Online Labs

- http://onlinelabs.in/anatomy

Biology

- http://studyjams.scholastic.com/studyjams/
- http://www.biointeractive/classroom-resources
- http://phet.colorado.edu/en/simulations/
  category/biology
- http://onlinelabs.in/biology
- http://scienceofeverydaylife.com
- http://www.csun.edu/science/software/simulations/
  simulations/.html

Chemistry

- http://phet.colorado.edu/en/simulations/
  category/chemistry
- http://onlinelabs.in/chemistry
- http://www.csun.edu/science/software/simulations/
  simulations/.html

Earth Science

- http://phet.colorado.edu/en/simulations/category/earth-science
- http://www.csun.edu/science/software/simulations/simulations/.html
- http://figurethis.nctm.org/index.html
- http://studyjams.scholastic.com/studyjams/
- http://illuminations.nctm.org/Games-Puzzles.aspx
- https://www.khanacademy.org
- www.arcademics.com

General

- https://learnzillion.com/
- http://www.sharemylesson.com/
- http://betterlesson.com/
- https://www.khanacademy.org/
- https://www.opened.io/
- http://www.gooru.org
- http://powermylearning.org/

Geology

- http://onlinelabs.in/geology

Language Arts

- https://bookopolis.com/

Physics

- http://phet.colorado.edu/en/simulations/category/physics
- www.hippocampus.org/Physics
- http://www.csun.edu/science/software/simulations/simulations/.html

Social Studies

- https://www.opensecrets.org
- http://www.politifact.com

(At the time of publication, these resources were active. For a current list of resources please visit my website at www.DrWendyOliver.com.)

APPENDIX E
CHECKLIST FOR CREDIBILITY OF ONLINE OR DISTANCE COURSES

☐ Is there an overview or course outline of the course?

☐ Are there tests, quizzes or assessments in the course?

☐ Is there a live teacher to help your child?

☐ Does your child have a user ID and password to access the course?

☐ Does your child have assigned timelines to complete the work? If so, what are they?

☐ Are there a begin and end dates for the course?

☐ Is the instructor of the course a qualified?

☐ If your child is a student-athlete, who plans to play collegiate sports, has the school submitted the course for approval to the NCAA?

☐ If your child is a student-athlete, who plans to play collegiate sports, have you discussed your child's goals of playing sports in college with a guidance counselor at the school?

☐ If your child is a student-athlete, who plans to play collegiate sports, is the coach at school aware that your child wants to play sports in college?

APPENDIX F
LITERACY STRATEGIES

Literacy Tips for Digital and Traditional Literacy Strategies

- Determine the purpose of the passage or piece of literature.
- Make connections about what you are reading and real life, your life, and classroom discussions.
  - Write those connections down on a sticky note, and put them on the page.
- Visualize what is going on as you read.
- Make predictions and anticipate what you think will happen next.
- Stop and think about what you read.
  - After you read each paragraph put it in your own words.
  - Can you connect what you just read to something you already know?
- Reread.
- Mark words you don't know, and look them up.

Digital Literacy Strategies

- Most importantly, in order to apply good digital literacy strategies your child or you needs to select credible websites. I have included a resource to help you do this.

- Apply all traditional literacy strategies listed above, but online you must be able to maneuver around the screen efficiently and with purpose. Stay focused on your mission! Don't get distracted by visual or elements or structural elements such as borders or flashing objects.

- Recognize page layout so as to decipher between headings, subheadings, tables, slides, transitions, text without distraction. This will help you stay focused.

- Recognize the difference in digital media such as SMS, Twitter, Facebook etc… In other words, know from where this type of information is coming. Know the differences in social networking updates vs. news updates, for example.

- If you have an e-reader, such as a Kindle, and you are reading a piece for school (chapter, article, book), then there may be a feature that will read aloud.

APPENDIX G
QUESTIONS FOR TEACHERS WITH A DIGITAL COMPONENT TO THE TRADITIONAL CLASSROOM

- Is there a website associated with the classroom? If so, where is it located? Get the link in writing or an email.

- Are my child's grades accessible electronically for viewing? Do I need a User ID and Password?

- Is there a calendar published with due dates for assignments? If so where is it located?

- Are their announcements made for the school or class digitally, and if so, where are they located?

- Is my child expected to submit any document electronically? If so, where and how? Are there written instructions that I can keep?

- Is the teacher accessible via email or text? If so, please provide communication information.

- What is the preferred method of communication? Digital, telephone?

- Is my child required to post or be active in any digital forums? If so, how often and where?

- Are there specific file types you will accept? If so, which types, and where can I find free copies of the required software or file conversions if I don't have them on my computer?

- Do you post assignments to the electronic community? If so, how often should my child monitor it?

REFERENCES

- 51 critical cyber-bullying statistics in 2019. *Broadband Search.* Retrieved from: https://www.broadbandsearch. net/blog/cyber-bullying-statistics

- Anderson, M., & Jiang, J. (2018, May). "Teens, social media, & technology." *Pew Research Center Internet & Technology.* Retrieved from: https://www.pewinternet. org/2018/05/31/teens-social-media-technology-2018/

- Asselin, S. B., & Mooney, M. (1996). *Diverse learners: Strategies for success.* Glen Allen, VA: Virginia Vocational Curriculum and Resource Center. (ED 406 529)

- Bergman, P. & Chan, E. (2019). Leveraging parents through low cost technology: The impact of high-frequency information on student achievement. Retrieved from http://www.columbia.edu/~psb2101/ ParentRCT.pdf

- Braiker, B. (2013). High-tech kids: Are they really smarter? *Parenting, 27*(1), 66-68.

- Carr, N. (2011). *The Shallows: What the Internet is doing to our brains.* New York, NY: W. W. Norton & Company.

- Child Rescue Network. (2019). Internet Safety. *Enough Is Enough: Making the Internet Safer for Children and Families.* Retrieved from: http://www.enough.org/stats_internet safety

- Child Rescue Network. (2019). Internet Safety. Retrieved from: http://childrescuenetwork.org/keeping-children-safe/internet-safety/

- Common core standards initiative: preparing America's students for college and career. (2018, August) Retrieved from http://www.corestandards.org/about-the-standards/development-process/

- Cooper, H. (2001). *The battle over homework* (2nd ed.). Thousand Oaks, CA: Corwin Press, Inc.

- Christensen, C., Johnson, C. W., & Horn, M. B. (2008). Disrupting class: How disruptive innovation will change the way the world learns. New York, NY: McGraw-Hill.

- Dillinger, J. (2018, March). Number of sex offenders by state. *World Atlas.* Retrieved from: https://www.

worldatlas.com/articles/state-by-state-numbers-of-registered-sex-offenders-in-the-us.html

- Dolot, Anna. (2018). The characteristics of Generation Z. e-mentor. 44-50. 10.15219/em74.1351.

- Echols, M. E. (2014). American workers are way behind. *Chief Learning Officer, 13*(2), 10.

- Elmore, T. (2012, February 8). A new generation of parents. Retrieved from http://www.howtolearn.com/2012/02/a-new-generation-of-parents/

- Fedock, B., & Young, E. (2013). Rethinking online writing and communication skills as a process: Teaching skills through interactive, learning style-based modeling. *Society for Information Technology & Teacher Education International Conference, 13*(1), *1291-1297.*

- Florence, F., & Hamilton, M. L. (2018). No more pencil: No more books. A district digital conversion. EdSurge (https://www.edsurge.com/n/2014-04-30-no-more-pencils-no-more-books-a-district-digital-conversion). Retrieved July 1, 2019.

- Friedman, J. (2018). Study: More students are enrolling in online courses. Retrieved from https://www.usnews.com/higher-education/online-education/articles/2018-01-11/study-more-students-are-enrolling-in-online-courses

- Ghose, T. (2016, October). Pediatricians: No more than 2 hours screen time daily for kids. *Scientific American.* Retrieved from: http://www.scientificamerican.com/article/pediatricians-no-more-than-2-hour-screen-time-kids/

- Grisham, D. L., & Wolsey, T.D. (2006). Re-centering the middle school classroom as a vibrant learning community: Students, literacy, and technology intersect. *Journal of Adult and Adolescent Literacy, 49*(8), 648-660.

- Horn, B., & Staker, H. (2014). *Blended: Using Disruptive Innovation to Improve Schools.* San Francisco, CA: Jossey-Bass.

- Jenson, F. E., & Nutt, A. E. (2016). *The Teenage Brain: A neuroscientist's survival guide to raising adolescents and young adults.* New York, NY: HarperCollins.

- Kanj, M., & Mitic, W. (2009). Health literacy and health promotion: Definitions, concepts and examples in the Eastern Mediterranean region. Retrieved from www.gchp7.info/resources/downloads/t1.pdf

- Kemp, J. (n.d.) *Parenting today's teenager.* Retrieved from http://www.parentingtodaysteenager.com. au/index.php

- Kinash, S., Wood, K., & Knight, D. (2013). Digital immigrant teachers and digital native students: What happens to teaching?, *Learning and Teaching Papers Paper, 50.* Retrieved from http://epublications.bond. edu.au/tls/50

- Kotchick, B. A., & Forehand, R. (2002). Putting parenting in perspective: A discussion of the contextual factors that shape parenting practices. *Journal of Child and Family Studies, 11*(3), 255-269.

- Lenhart, A. (2007, June). Cyberbullying and Online Teens. Pew Research Center & Internet Technology. Retrieved from www.pewinternet.org/2007/06/27/ cyberbullying

- Lenhart A. (2009, December). Teens and sexting. *Pew Research Center & Internet Technology.* Retrieved from www.pewinternet.org/2009/12/15/teens-and-sexting.

- Lenhart, A. (2010, February). Social media and young adults. *Pew Research Center Internet & Technology.*

Retrieved from www.pewinternet.org/2010/02/03/
social-media-and-young-adults/

- Levin, D., & Arafeh, S. (2002). The digital
  disconnect: The widening gap between internet-
  savvy students and their schools. *Washington, DC:
  Pew Internet & American Life Project*, August 14,
  2002. Report, 67, 20. Retrieved from http://www.
  pewinternet.org/~/media/Files/Reports/2002/PIP_
  Schools_Internet_Report.pdf.pdf

- Miller, M. (2011, October, 5). *Understanding
  Generation Z: The Facebook generation.* Retrieved
  from http://www.quepublishing.com/articles/article.
  aspx?p=1753977

- National Forum on Educational Statistics, (2006).
  Forum guide to elementary/secondary education (NFES
  2006-803). Washington, DC: US Department of
  Education, National Forum on Education Statistics.

- NCAA Eligibility Center. Retrieved from: www.
  eligibilitycenter.org

- Netsmartz. Retrieved from: http://www.netsmartz.
  org/safety/statistics#_ftnref8

- Organization for Economic Cooperation and
  Development (2012), *Literacy, Numeracy and Problem*

Solving in Technology-Rich Environments: Framework for the OECD Survey of Adult Skills. Paris, France: OECD Publishing. doi: 10.1787/9789264128859-en

• Oliver, Wendy L., "Investigating whether a value-added teaching effectiveness model designed for traditional classrooms can be used to measure online teaching quality" (2010). *Masters Theses and Doctoral Dissertations.* https://scholar.utc.edu/theses/353

• Online predators – statistics. Retrieved from: http://www.puresight.com/Pedophiles/Online-Predators/online-predators-statistics.html

• Parr, B. (2010, October). "The average teenager sends 3,339 texts per month STATS." *Mashable.* Retrieved from https://mashable.com/2010/10/14/nielsen-texting-stats/#PTJrTxmueSqz

• Paton, G. (2014, April). Infant unable to use toy building blocks due to iPad addiction. *The Telegraph.* Retrieved from http://www.telegraph.co.uk/education/educationnews/10767878/Infants-unable-to-use-toy-building-blocks-due-to-iPad-addiction.html

- Rideout, V. (2018). *Zero to eight: Children's media use in America*. San Francisco, CA: Common Sense Media. Retrieved from http://www.commonsensemedia.org/sites/default/files/research/zerotoeightfinal2018.pdf

- Rideout, V.M.A. & Robb, M.B (2018). Social media, social lives: Teens reveal their experiences. Common Sense Media Retrieved from https://www.commonsensemedia.org/research/social-media-social-life-2018

- Roblyer, M. D., & Doering, A. (2013). *Integrating educational technology into teaching* (6th ed.). Upper Saddle River, NJ: Pearson.

- Roizen, M. F., & Oz, M. C. (2010). *You raising your child*. New York, NY: Simon & Schuster, Inc.

- Rozario, B. (2011, April 4). How to parent Gen Y and Z. Retrieved from http://parenthots.com/features/How-to-parent-Gen-Y-and-Z.aspx

- Sales, N. J. (2016). *American girls, social media and the secret lives of teenagers*. New York, NY: Penguin Random House.

- Schroer, W. (2004, April 16). *Generations X, Y, Z and the others*. *The Social Librarian*. Retrieved from http://www.socialmarketing.org/newsletter/features/generation3.htm

- Scrutinizing data privacy policies of Edmodo, Khan, and Pearson. (2014, April). Retrieved from https://www.edsurge.com/n/2014-04-14-scrutinizing-data-privacy-policies-of-edmodo-khan-and-pearson

- Shuler, C. (2012). *iLearn II: An analysis of the education category of the iTunes app store.* New York, NY: The Joan Ganz Cooney Center at Sesame Workshop. Retrieved from http://joanganzcooneycenter.org/upload_kits/ilearnii.pdf

- Taylor, M. (2004). Generation NeXT comes to college: Meeting the postmodern student. [Monograph]. Retrieved from http://www.lib.wayne.edu/sites/accreditation/examples/documents/generationnext.pdf

- United States. National Commission on Excellence in Education. (1983). A nation at risk: The imperative for educational reform: A report to the Nation and the Secretary of Education, United States Department of Education. Washington, D.C.: The Commission: [Supt. of Docs., U.S. G.P.O. distributor].

- Usdan, J., & Almasy, K. (2012). FCC Chairman Announces Jobs-Focused Digital Literacy Partnership

Between Connect2Compete and the 2,800 American Job Centers. Retrieved from https://www.fcc.gov/news-events/blog/2012/07/23/fcc-chairman-announces-jobs-focused-digital-literacy-partnership-between

- Weinberger, J. W. (2017). *The boogeyman exists: And he's in your child's back pocket* (2nd ed.). Self-Published, United States: Weinberger.

69045690R00099

Made in the USA
Middletown, DE
25 September 2019